Victory
Goes to the Business with Superior Systems

A How to Guide to Transform Your Business and Your Life Through Systems **by Brad Miller**

The opinions expressed in this manuscript are solely the opinions of the author and do not represent the opinions or thoughts of the publisher. The author has represented and warranted full ownership and/or legal right to publish all the materials in this book.

Victory Goes to The Business With Superior Systems
How to Transform Your Business and Your Life Through Systems
All Rights Reserved.
Copyright © 2014 Brad Miller
v2.0

Cover Photo © 2014 Brad Miller. All rights reserved - used with permission.

This book may not be reproduced, transmitted, or stored in whole or in part by any means, including graphic, electronic, or mechanical without the express written consent of the publisher except in the case of brief quotations embodied in critical articles and reviews.

Outskirts Press, Inc.
http://www.outskirtspress.com

ISBN: 978-1-4787-3503-8

Outskirts Press and the "OP" logo are trademarks belonging to Outskirts Press, Inc.

PRINTED IN THE UNITED STATES OF AMERICA

This book is dedicated to my best friend, my high school sweetheart and my life partner.

I am blessed because I got to marry her. Crystal, "Many women do noble things, but you surpass them all."

Contents

Preface Do you need to read this book? xi
- *A 15 question survey to test your Systems Savvy*
- *Get Your Systems Savvy Score*

Introduction "Mr. Miller, please help!" xvi
- *How I would've helped Marta's sons*
- *Business is hard and complex – everything must be systemized and documented*
- *Your business apart from you, not a part of you*

Chapter 1 My Mess Becomes My Message 1
  The journey from chaos to a business that works

  "I can easily imagine a life without a business – but I can't imagine a business without a life."
  - Michael Gerber, *The E-Myth*

- *My journey from chaos to order*
- *How to have a business and a life*
- *Not a career change, but a belief system change*
- *Expect more from your business...and get it!*
- *What's your victory?*

Chapter 2 Systems Create Order from Chaos 14
Becoming the Intelligent Designer of your business

"It is best to do things systematically, since we are only human and disorder is our worst enemy."
 – Hesiod

- Order: the sign of Intelligent Design
- What exactly is a system?
- "If you can't replicate the process you can't duplicate the success"
- Your McDonald's field trip and systems recon mission

Chapter 3 Fall In Love with Systems 26
17 Beautiful Benefits of Systems

"The Success is in the System."
 - AT&T

- Ramping up - making your business scalable
- Why you can (and should) hire attitude over ability
- How systems drastically reduce your #1 cost – labor
- Create extraordinary systems for your ordinary people

Chapter 4 Micro-Manage Your Business... to the Max... 33
Systems designed to create a business that works... without you

"Delegation without Systemization is Frustration."
 - Brad Miller

- Micro-manage is not a dirty word
- Why you must micro-manage every detail of your business vision
- The business owner as creator and inventor
- "Scripting" the customer experience from beginning to end

Chapter 5 Recipes for Success 39
   Systemizing the Order Fulfillment Process

   "If you can't measure it, you can't manage it."
   - Peter Drucker

- *Why recipes are systems that give you control*
- *How to replicate the process to duplicate the success*
- *How to get your business out of your employee's head*
- *How to build systems around your promises*
- *13 Order Fulfillment systems you can adapt and use*

Chapter 6 Stop Random Acts of Marketing – Start Creating Marketing Systems 50
   Systemizing the Lead Generation Process

   "If you can't create a system that brings you a sufficient quantity and quality of leads on a continual and steady basis, you can't control your business."
   - Dan Kennedy

- *Why your inside reality and outside perception don't match*
- *Why you simply must become a marketing expert!*
- *Why marketing is not selling – and selling is not marketing*

Chapter 7 Knowing Your Numbers 62
   Systemizing the Management and Measuring Process

   "Whatever you measure, improves."
   - Peter Drucker

- *How to measure what matters - Key Performance Indicators*
- *How to create simple business dashboards*
- *Why knowing your numbers moves the profit needle*

Chapter 8 Your Life and Your Business Imagined: *The Value of Vision PART I*..................................... 68

Create the vision of the *life* you want, then create a business that makes that life reality

> *"Where there is no vision the people perish."*
> *- Proverbs 29:18*

- How to create a business that gives you life
- Why the Vision must come before the systems
- How your Vision can create tasks for your team
- My pitfalls of working without a Vision
- A greenhouse operation "Tournament Ready"

Chapter 9 Your Life and Your Business Vision Becoming Reality: *The Value of Vision Part II*................... 75

From Big Vision to Daily Tasks and Systems

> *"Write the vision; make it plain on tablets, so he may run who reads it."*
> *- Habakkuk 2:2*

- The Inverted Pyramid – Breaking it all down
- Why you need vision statements for every division
- What are the businesses within your business?
- Why every division has their own 37 (more or less) systems
- Target Times and "fixing" Parkinson's Law
- Now let's go Design and Innovate every task

Chapter 10 11 Rules and Reminders for Designing and Innovating Your Systems 90

"Your systems are perfectly designed for the results you're getting."
- *Pat Morley*

- A get-the-kids-dressed-in-the-morning system – really?
- Don't just systemize the process – innovate it
- My epiphany visit to Papa John's Pizza
- Vince Lombardi's blocking and tackling systems
- Everyone Knows Where Everything Goes systems

Chapter 11 Making your Systems Stick 103
The Systems for the Systems

"What you tolerate, you encourage. What you permit, you promote."
- *Unknown*

- Condo-commando or business professional?
- How to stop encouraging non-compliance
- The magic of a Strategic Training Objectives checklist
- Everything's falling apart and you don't know it
- System fixes for The Deception of the Gradual

Chapter 12 The Narrow Road to a Business that Works 114
Entering the funnel backwards

"Entrepreneurship is living a few years of your life like most people won't, so that you can spend the rest of your life like most people can't"
   - Anonymous

"Small is the gate and narrow the road that leads to life and only a few find it."
   - Jesus of Nazareth

- *How to choose the business that will serve your life*
- *How to not only encourage your team – but equip them*
- *How to find the latent opportunity locked in your business and industry*
- *Why the narrow road really is the path to success and freedom*

Acknowledgments 124

PREFACE

Do you need to read this book?

A 15 question survey to test your Systems Savvy

Stop! Do you need to read this book? Don't invest your time reading this book (or any book) if it won't make a significant contribution to your life.

This book is designed for the small business owner or general manager who is frustrated that their business is not working as well as it should and knows there must be a better way. Take this 15 question survey and then score yourself.

4 = Strongly Agree

3 = Agree

2 = Disagree

1 = Strongly Disagree

1) ____ I am enjoying my work-life because I have a business that serves my life and does not rob me of life.

2) ____ I arrive for work when it is convenient for me because the business does not depend on me directly supervising the staff.

3) ____ I am investing significant time on improving and revolutionizing the customer experience systems.

4) ____ Every person on my staff knows exactly what to do when they arrive for work and they get busy with getting it done.

5) ____ The work of the business (the customer experience: from prospect, to order fulfillment, to referrals) is systemized and documented (written down in manuals).

6) ____ I am involved in the business, doing the work for which I am uniquely gifted and enjoy most – and have delegated all other tasks to my staff.

7) ____ The operational details of the business are not in my head (or in an employee's head) but are completely detailed in systems manuals.

8) ____ I am excited because my business is scalable and growing – new customers are welcomed and seamlessly integrated.

9) ___New installations and/or service calls are executed with precision because my systems, forms, and procedures are deliberate and followed.

10) ___I regularly invest time in innovating the order fulfillment, customer service, and marketing functions of my business – "I am working 'on' the business as the inventor and not 'in' the business as an employee."

11) ___My lead generation system consistently fills our sales pipeline with prospects attracted by our unique marketing message.

12) ___My marketing systems are automated and provide compelling follow-up that is educating our prospects about our company.

13) ___My lead conversion is driven by sales systems and scripts that deliver a persuasive message and close the sale.

14) ___I have a system for finding, hiring, training, and inspiring people that are ideally suited for each position in our business.

15) ___I have a dashboard system that tracks the critical numbers of our operation including sales, finances, customer service, and order fulfillment.

Score Your Business and Your Life

15 to 30 - I feel your pain, business friend. You're wearing your business like a ball and chain and it stopped being fun a long time ago. Be of good courage; there is hope for a brighter and more fulfilling future, because there is a path that leads you to a better business and a fuller life.

This book will transform your business and your life! Read on, take notes and implement like crazy.

31 to 34 - You've tasted the sweetness of some days when your business was firing on all cylinders...but those days don't happen often. You're probably still working in your business full time as a key employee and without your presence, things quickly deteriorate. You need a vacation but are scared to death to take one.

This book will transform your business and your life because you already know what to do; you need help to do it more consistently - and systematically.

45 to 55 - You've obviously invested a lot of effort working ON your business, but you settle for less than what your business could be. You need to renew your vision of creating a business that really works, a business that works without your daily presence and input, a business that serves people (and you) in amazing ways.

This book will help you in immensely practical ways to get "fired up and inspired" to run for the finish line. Read on, and rekindle the vision that brought you this far.

56 to 60 - Congratulations! You have a great handle on your business and business systems. You are an inventor and an innovator and have worked on your business hard and long. You now have discretionary time to invest in other projects, businesses, and worthy causes of your liking. You're probably reading this book on a beach or somewhere else where you do your best work.

This book will be a confirmation of your current belief systems and work! Read on and then give a copy to a friend.

INTRODUCTION

"Mr. Miller, please, my two son's small business needs your help!"

Plain and simple, my business was a mess - as a result, my life was also a mess. As determined as I was to make my business a success, I was feeling like a victim every time my company added another customer – crazy, I know.

This was certainly not the life I expected when I had the idea to start my own business. The business was consuming me, it was a heavy burden that seemed impossible to unload. The combination of my cockiness and naiveté left me completely unprepared for just how hard it would be to start a business from scratch.

If any of that sounds remotely familiar, you are exactly in the right place, reading the right book. This book is designed for you, to throw you a lifeline, and to give you hope for a different reality. The book starts with parts of my own journey – the journey from a business that was consuming my life, to a business that was (and is) enriching my life. There is a path

> **The combination of my cockiness and naiveté left me completely unprepared for just how hard it would be to start a business from scratch.**

out of the chaos and anxiety of running a small business that's always on the edge in one way or another. Yes, there is a path and I'll do my best to describe it in this book step-by-step, and in very practical terms.

The idea for this book had been on my To-Do list for a long time, but one morning on my regular walk I got the nudge I needed to make it a priority and get it on the Done list.

My walk had actually turned into a new «start the day right system.» Instead of shuffling around for 15 or 20 minutes with a cup of coffee, I had begun starting the day with a two-mile walk. It was an idea I got from reading a random blog - and now I was hooked. As quickly as possible, after getting out of bed, I put on my shoes and shorts and headed out the door - my mind waking up while walking. It›s a habit now and I look forward to the early exercise and thinking time.

This particular morning, my mind was racing with ideas for writing a book. It was a book I'd had on my mind for a while – about how I had transformed my interior plant business by learning how to create systems.

But on this morning I saw the exact outline and the subject of each chapter as clear as day. It would be a step-by-step guide from frustration and chaos (how most business owners live) to an orderly and methodical business operation. The book I saw was partly autobiographical about my own journey from the brink of almost giving up my small business because it was just too hard and I couldn't figure out how to make it better or easier.

I became more and more convinced that this was a good idea and a worthy project - a real business book for small business people

XVIII ✿ VICTORY GOES TO THE BUSINESS WITH SUPERIOR SYSTEMS

like me - people that love practical advice and real-world experience to truly do business better.

My pace quickened as I headed home to get in front of my laptop so I could capture everything I was thinking about as soon as possible. For 30 or 40 minutes I transcribed everything in a flurry of typing. It came so easily and naturally that my typing skill (make that lack of) was the only thing slowing me down. When I was satisfied that I got everything down, I sat back, sighed, and took a mental break.

I checked my email and found a plea for help from a woman named Marta.*

Months earlier, I was a guest on Gail Ross's television show called, *"Testimonies of Triumph."* Gail is a vibrant, Christian woman who loves to share stories about triumph. Her guests share how God helped them overcome difficult situations of all kinds.

Gail, who also loves marketplace ministry (Christian influence in the business world), thought my story of small business growth and come-from-behind triumph was worth telling. Today when I tell my business start-up story, my common phrase, with as much candidness as possible, is "the only thing I knew less about than plants was business." It's true!

Marta was watching the episode of *Testimonies of Triumph* that aired the night before and something I said gave her hope. She was a widow and her two grown sons had a business that was struggling. She knew they needed help, but had no idea of what or who or how.

Since Gail had aired my email address at the end of the show, Marta decided to ask for my help - below is her email as she wrote it:

> **From:** JMMERR [mailto:ziXXXXXXXXXXXXX]
> **Sent:** Thursday, September 13, 8:12 PM
> **To:** bradmillerips@comcast.net
> **SSSubject:** Mr.Miller please my two sons small business needs your Help.
>
> Dear Mr. Miller,
>
> I saw you on TV @ 7 pm today & you said you are in marketplace ministry. I have two boys that open a small business which I observe they need a Christian guidance to guide them or give an advice, from a successful Christian businessman like you, please let me know if you can help them, in the name of God I beg you to GIVE them direction with God's help & guidance PLEASE, You can contact me, Marta Marion my email is Zinxxxxx@xxxxxxx.com tel# is 123- 555 - 1212 - ,please let me know if you can help, Your consideration is most appreciated ,please let me hear from you. May the Divine assistance remains with you always. Respectfully yours, Marta Marion

* (name changed to protect privacy)

Oh my goodness, I thought, this is exactly what I had in mind for my book: a book of practical advice to help guys like this. Wow, *what a coincidence!* No, of course not, this was my "God nudge" to do what I had been thinking about doing for years. The Divine timing of my walk and book idea combined with the email from Marta was the kick-start I needed. Now I was convinced; it was a matter of obedience and not preference.

My heart ached for Marta and for the small business her boys were striving and struggling to maintain. I could share in their frustration and possibly yours, with having a small business that was taking over your life and not doing what a business should do - add to your life. The emotion that overflowed from Marta's email was just too familiar to me, *"in the name of God I beg you to GIVE them direction with God's help & guidance...PLEASE."* Yes, familiar because I had cried out in very similar ways and prayed asking for this same kind of help, "God help me, this is too hard, I can't do this anymore and I want to quit."

Obviously, I thought of everything I had just typed minutes before - This is it! This is exactly what I would share with Marta's sons.

If I had the chance to meet with her sons - which I never did, I would invite them to Bob Evans restaurant, then over coffee and breakfast give them my story of **how I came from a business that was stealing my life away, to a business that was giving me life**.

There is a path out of the mess that Marta's sons and so many other small businesses find themselves trapped in. There is a way out of the chaos, frustration, and randomness - towards control and intentionality. It's possible to have a business that works and runs smoothly, and gives you life, income, options, and choices. That was my journey, my story – and I love to tell it.

Listen, small business friend, your pain and frustration with your business is not unique. It's very probable that you are suffering from the weight of your own *success:* you love what you do and because you serve your customers well, you have your hands full with more than you could possibly get done and none of your employees know how to do "it" as proficiently as you do.

This book is for you to learn how to correct that exact problem.

Your business doesn't have to rely on you knowing and doing everything yourself. Your business can be a beautifully orchestrated and predictable arrangement of systems, all working together to serve people in meaningful ways. You can enjoy your business! You can be thankful for your business and your customers – not hate them both.

Business is not easy, business is hard. But your business can be a "good hard." It can be a difficult mountain that you climb and you can enjoy the journey and relish the accomplishment. You can be on top of your business and feel victorious, rather than feeling the heavy weight of your business bearing down on you. I know...I've lived both.

Business is not only challenging, business is complicated. Contrary to popular belief, complicated is not bad – complicated is good! If business was easy and straightforward everyone would do it and you don't want that kind of competition. Business has lots of moving parts that make it complicated, and that's precisely **why everything *(every thing)* must be systemized and documented.**

The transformation begins when you start thinking differently about your business – thinking of it as *apart from you, not a part of you!*

> **Everything *(every thing)* must be systemized and documented.**

You must expect more and demand more from your business or you will never take control of your business. No, you don't have to be an employee in your own business (unless you want to). Yes, you can decide upon the life you want to live and then go work on your

XXII ✪ VICTORY GOES TO THE BUSINESS WITH SUPERIOR SYSTEMS

business to create the life you've imagined. Yes, it's a journey and it will take time, but the journey has a path, and I, along with many others, have discovered that path. I want to be your guide on this journey and show you the way. I want to be candid and transparent; there's a lot to be learned from mistakes – so learn from the mistakes I've made.

I want to be both practical and real-world. Let's sidestep even the hint of theory or speculation. Our journey together will be from my "expensive experience" of trial and error which led to trial and success.

<u>You must want it!</u>

I'm ready if you are. But you must be committed to the journey and you must truly want it. No one else can want it for you, including the people that love you the most – <u>not even your mother.</u>

Boy do I wish my story about Marta and her boys had a better ending. I would love to tell you how I met her sons and taught them the step-by-step process for creating systems for their business. I'd love to tell you that story, but I never met them. They never contacted me. If someone has given you this book because "they" think you need it, stop now. The systems development process will not happen because someone else sees that your business needs help. You must want it for yourself.

I was really looking forward to that Bob Evans breakfast, but it never happened - I wasn't able to help Marta's sons. I did send Marta back an email - but told her she must have her sons call me:

"Hi Marta – so good to hear from you – and Thank You for your kind words. Small business is tough – and without God's

help it is even harder. I would be happy to talk with your sons and give them some guidance. If they are interested, please have them call my office and give their name to my assistant Dawn. They should tell her that they are Marta's son and leave a phone number where I can call them back. Have one of your sons call my number if "they" are interested. Please don't call for them – they must want the help."

I never heard from Marta's sons. But Marta and her sons did serve me well while writing this book. They, all three, kept me real. "What exactly would these guys need to know to really make their business go?" "What change would Marta need to see in the business <u>and</u> lives of her sons to give her peace and joy?"

In a nutshell, "How exactly could I have best helped them?"

The answer to that question is this book! The answer to their business problems is in my experience a systems strategy, hence the name *"Victory Goes to the Business with Superior Systems."* You, will get my step-by-step journey out of my own business mess, and into a business of order, hence the sub-title, *"A 'How To Guide' to Transform Your Business And Your Life Through Systems."*

So again, this is not a book on "systems theory" or what you might hear in a university MBA course.

Yes, Marta and her sons kept me from being fanciful and abstract because I've had them in mind as I've been writing. But also I've had **you** in mind. A small business person (owner or general manager), like me, who wants to have a real business that thrives and works extremely well, so that.....and this is the big idea...so that you can have an amazing life of love, service, family, friends, and personal fulfillment. In short, a business *and* a life.

So let's have breakfast at Bob Evan's – sit, drink coffee, and talk about exactly what you have to do to create the successful business that you imagined when the idea first blossomed in your mind.

CHAPTER 1

My Mess Becomes My Message

The journey from chaos to a business that works

"I can easily imagine a life without a business – but I can't imagine a business without a life."

- **Michael Gerber,** *The E-Myth*

The conversation with my cousin Brent, at his Indiana lake home, was the first real clue that my business wasn't what it could be or what it should be - and worse, that I wouldn't be happy doing it for much longer.

Brent, a CPA and partner in a large firm, is the consummate business man and our conversations always come around to business. He was the first one that helped me to see the uniqueness of my company and the huge benefit of growing my "Monthly Recurring Revenue."

He said to me at an earlier time, "Brad, the benefit of your business is the fact that you can build annuity income instead of just transactional income." Since, I had absolutely no idea what that meant or why it was important, I said what any young business guy would say, "Ah, yeah right, I know what you mean Brent."

That's a topic for later, but a vital one at that. Monthly recurring revenue is king in any small business. You start the month not "having to" make a sale, knowing your expenses are covered; it's called predictable income. It's the most important number we track and the one we seek to build our most comprehensive systems around.

> *"I really don't want any more customers - every time I add another customer, I feel like I am giving up another piece of my life."*

This time though, Brent and I were talking about marketing, sales, and adding new customers, when I said something that I can't even believe now. I said, "I really don't want any more customers - every time I add another customer, I feel like I am giving up another piece of my life." That was exactly what I said and back then I really meant it! Today, we celebrate new sales and new customers with high-fives and ringing the cow bell. But back then it was a totally different story.

Looking back on that moment of transparency with my cousin, and verbalizing how I really felt, should have been a huge wake-up call - but the problems in my business occurred to me much slower and took more pain and frustration for me to actually want to make a change.

The truth is though, that what I'd just stated in that moment of clarity with my cousin was the reality. Every time I added a new customer, the business didn't get better or easier - it got harder and demanded much more of me.

Does that sound even a little familiar? Perhaps you're like I was - a victim of your own success and hard work. The pattern for many, if not most, small businesses is the same. You start the business with a lot of energy and the commitment to do whatever it takes, to make it go - and go it does. You hire some people to help you but don't really train them because there's no such animal as a systems manual. So *you* are still the go-to guy or gal for practically everything. Then, because you're the only one that really knows everything, your day is filled with the day-to-day operations, and your personal capacity to do any more leads to frustration and burn out!

My friend, if you feel trapped, there's a way out of the chaos - there is a far better way to do business, and to live life. Today I have something of inestimable value - I have a business that works. More importantly, I have a business that works without me. Today, I can say I know how truly valuable and desirable this is - because I used to have a business that didn't work - and took everything from me.

My passion and my desire in writing this book is to show you that you can have a transformed business plus a better and more satisfying life. Yes, I want to inspire you too and for you to know that you can do this. You can create a business that adds to your life instead of robbing you of life.

I can easily imagine a life without a business - but I can›t imagine a business without a life. – Michael Gerber

What this quote means is there are lots of happy and content people living their lives without business ownership; they have jobs.

But the option you want to avoid, at all costs, is having a business and nothing else. No family life, no friends, no recreational life; just a business that controls all your time and attention.

You don't have to settle. You can have it all: a business and a life. A full, rich life of love and a family, friends, and work - work that you enjoy and that you're the best at! But the journey to creating a business that works is just that - a journey, and not a short one.

Yes, I want to inspire you because you'll need to be inspired, encouraged, and reminded of the benefits you'll receive if you commit wholeheartedly to this process. The business development process. Let me share my story of frustration to inspiration and ultimately to what we're going to talk about most - systemization.

Light dawns in a dark tunnel

I started my company, Interior Plant Scapes, in 1983 when I was 22 years old. My confession now is that the only thing I knew less about than plants, was business. My dad had acquired a small piece of property behind our home and then enlisted the free labor of my two brothers and me to landscape and beautify it. Sunday afternoons meant church first, then yard work, then freedom to go to the beach. But what was duty became joy as I developed an interest and love for plants - especially potted plants.

After our back patio was full of potted plants, they started heading to my bedroom. It was normal then, but seems weird now that as a teenager I had a 7 foot Dieffenbachia in the corner of my bedroom...not an easy plant, and I had grown it from a seedling.

Longing to follow in my Dad's entrepreneurial example, I always knew I wanted my own business - just wasn't sure what. After a close shave with the catering business – which, now I am so glad didn't work out, I heard about the professional plant care business.

The interior-scape industry, which got its start in the late 70s, was now booming in the early 80s and though still a novel idea, seemed the perfect business for me.

When you're 22 and full of energy - and yourself - the idea of starting a business from scratch seemed like no big deal. How hard could it be? So I started waiting tables at night and worked in my business during the day. Note that was working "in" my business. As the only employee I did everything!

The answer to, "how hard could it be?" came soon enough. Answer: "really hard." Selling and getting new accounts was the hardest part. Selling is difficult to begin with, but even harder for a 22 year old with no formal sales training, selling a new business idea. "What, you want me to lease live plants?"

Through perseverance and a lot of trial and error (I actually have a degree from T and E University) Interior Plant Scapes grew and after 14 months I was able to quit my restaurant job because I had reached my goal, $200 a week in take-home pay from the business. Yes, these were tough years, the early years of growing my company from one $40 a month account (thank you Dr. Fox) to five and then ten and then twenty accounts. Then, I added my first employee, and later a second. It was not that the work was hard; I've always enjoyed hard work and the satisfaction that comes from a "good tired" at the end of a project or a laborious day. The challenging work of small business ownership is working without a plan and working without clarity of priorities. For me it was the unrelenting physical, mental, and emotional strain of too many plates spinning all the time and never knowing which one was going to drop next.

Help, I want out

Finally I got to the point where I thought there must be a better way - this is just too hard. The change though was not the one I was looking for. Our church had just gone through a one month course based on Rick Warren's book The Purpose Driven Life and I was honestly asking myself some tough questions about what kind of work I really enjoyed, and wanted to devote my life to. Big questions such as, "what is my life about" and "what is really important?"

Through the curriculum our church was using, I learned about a course called, Life Plan. It was a two day intensive look at your life whereby you learn your passions, gifts, and temperament to point you toward your best career fit. Through this Life Plan course I learned a lot about myself, but the most interesting discovery I made that weekend was that I possessed the skills, aptitude, and temperament for a career in consulting.

That was exciting for me because I was so unhappy in my business I seriously started to pursue the opportunity of becoming a consultant. Yes, you heard me right - I had a small business that was not fun anymore, it was consuming my life; I didn't want any new customers, and I didn't see a way to make it better. It was the classic case of "those who can't do, teach."

I wanted to become a consultant to other business people and help them make their businesses better - but the problem was I didn't know how to make mine better.

The training event I attended was a Strategic Planning workshop led by Tom Patterson. The course was for high level CEO's and consultants who wanted to learn how to implement and/or train others in the Strategic Planning process.

True to form for most business seminars and conferences, the best take-aways come from the conversations in the hallway on break and not in the sessions. During a break I met one of the speakers, Bob Shanks. Bob was the epitome of the stereotypical California cool guy: handsome, fit, tan, and smart about business - he even had a red convertible Mustang - I wanted to be him. Bob was a former small business owner who sold his business and now helped teach other business owners and leaders. He was genuinely interested in me and asked great questions about my life and business.

Bob recommended some great business books and said things like, "you need to start working on your business and not just in it," and "get your business out of your head and onto paper and document your systems, so that your business can operate in the hands of others without your day to day involvement."

Bob was quoting *Michael Gerber*, the author of **The E-Myth**, a book you'll hear me reference and quote quite a bit (and which you should buy and read). Bob's advice along with this book and many others, gave me the first glimmer of hope that my business could be something different, something much better than what I had.

> **I had been looking for a change, a career change - but what I ultimately needed was a belief system change.**

That conversation with Bob changed my life and gave me a new attitude about my business. I had been looking for a change, a career change, but what I ultimately needed was a belief system change. **I** needed to *think* differently about my business.

Reread that last sentence, it's extremely important. You need to think differently about business because until you believe that your business and your life can be different, you won't change. **Your life changes the moment you begin to think differently about your business** because you have at that instant begun to expect more from your business.

My friend, that's huge, because most small business professionals stop far short of what their businesses can do for them (and for others) not to mention the improved lifestyle and standard of living it can give them.

Begin now to ***think differently*** about your business – *"As you believe, so shall it be done to you."*

Begin now to ***expect more*** from your business – your life and your business will rise (or fall) to the level of your expectations.

Begin now to ***tolerate less*** from your business – "Whatever you tolerate you encourage." We'll unpack that quote more later, but know now that whatever you tolerate and let slide, you encourage and say by your silence, "that's OK, you're meeting our standards."

> **Your life changes the moment you begin to think differently about your business.**

The core idea of the *The E Myth* is that your business should run like a franchise, of a highly successful prototype operation. In short, your business and all of its functions should be systemized. This here is the quote from Michael Gerber that I memorized and now hangs on my office wall:

"All extraordinarily successful businesses are Systems - totally integrated systems which work in a systematically logical and consistent manner. A manner which can be described - systems which can be duplicated."

My friend, that's not how most small business owners think about their business and it's not their expectation. However, that's exactly what I want to simplify and share with you. You can have that kind of business...you can have an "extraordinarily successful business."

The systems development process, the process I am going to describe in the simplest terms possible, is the way out of the chaos you find yourself trapped in. It is the guide to the life you have dreamed; a life filled with choices of "get to's" versus "have-to's."

Dare to dream about the life you really want to live and go to work creating the business that makes that dream a reality. That dream will serve you well as you invest in the work ahead.

Work where you want to

One of my personal goals of having a business that works was this: work where I – and when I want to, doing the work I wanted to do. When I finally caught the vision for how improving my business could improve my life, I created a new goal. The work that I discovered I loved to do most at that time was working "on" the business. And my favorite place to be was in the mountains of North Carolina in the summer and the beaches of South West Florida in the winter.

The dream and goal that inspired me was to be able to do the work I really loved to do (working "on" the business), doing it where I really wanted to do it, the mountains of North Carolina - and doing it when I wanted to do it, in the months of June, July and August when the weather in Florida is sweltering and humid.

My wife, Crystal, loves the mountains too and agreed this would be a great goal. If you've been in the mountains of North Carolina in July and August, you know why - the weather is gorgeous and the views are breath-taking. It doesn't take much to imagine why I'd want to do my work up there.

Having this goal, a three to five year goal for us, was just the thing I needed to push me towards the finish line. It started to prepare me and just as important, prepare my staff for a time when I would not be present on a day-to-day basis. That became the assumption - the boss is not in the office. It really helped all of us to have a different perspective on how our business should work; namely, it should work systematically.

Just because I could spend a couple of months away from my business didn't mean the systems development process was completed and that my franchise proto-type business model was done. It was a milestone on the journey and a rewarding one at that, but the biggest benefit was having my belief system turned to reality: having a business work without you was possible.

The biggest lesson from reaching that first milestone of "summers in the mountains," was the realization of how important it was for me personally to get out of the business to really see the opportunities. By stepping out of the day-to-day operations I got a new view (literally a 5000 foot view in the Blue Ridge Mountains) of my business. With head-down and agenda full, I was not seeing the possibilities for making my business better. Your mind needs to relax and refresh to really soar. There's a story about Joe Kennedy and his experience away from his business that I heard a speaker tell. Kennedy was reported to have said, "I never made any real money until I was sitting around the pool in Miami Beach." Lots of funny comebacks to that one, but the point is clear – if you're wound up tight inside your business all the time working "in" it, you'll miss the goldmine of working "on" it. Don't get me wrong, there are still lots of ways to work on making your business better while you're working to fulfill orders – but it's amazing what you can achieve when you get away and intentionally THINK about your business.

What's Your Victory?

My first victory was the freedom to spend the summer in the mountains of North Carolina as a business owner, instead of being in Florida working as an employee. What's your victory? What does victory mean for your business – and more importantly, your life?

In chapter eight you'll read about The Value of Vision. You'll learn that you really can create the vision of the life you want, then create a business that makes that life a reality. Right now, you may believe you're light years away from a business that works without you – and you may be mired in the day-to-day muck of survival mode mentality. Keep the faith – victory can be yours! So again I'll ask, "What's your victory and what's the vision of the life you want?" You must prepare for the victory, plan for the victory and expect the victory, because I'm going to show you step-by-step how to make it happen. It's not magical and it's not mysterious – rather it's systematic.

Victory Goes to the Business with Superior Systems

This book really is a how to guide to transform your business and your life through systems – and that rightly leads to amazing victories. So are you ready? Will you commit to the journey? Will you commit to the process of digging into and thinking deeply about every detail of the business you own so that you can systemize it?

If you do here are the victories you can rightfully expect:

1. The Victory of ...a business that works – it works like it should without the chaos and call backs and dropped balls.

2. The Victory of ...a business that works without you – you are not an employee; you are the owner, the creator and the innovator. What fun!

3. The Victory of ...a business that is differentiated from the competition so that you are never an apples to apples comparison (apples to oranges is the way you want your customers and prospects to think of you). Your business defies comparison.

4. The Victory of ...*serving people* in deep and meaningful ways with a product/service they love and willingly pay for (you love your customers and they love you).

5. The Victory of ...having a business *and* a life – a life to do the work you were really created to do and a life to pursue the dream that is still inside of you.

6. The Victory of ...business and personal income that is predictable and regular.

Have a business AND a life

7. The Victory of ...business and personal income that is above average – stop working for less than your hourly employees!

8. The Victory of ...a business that does not depend on one key employee who has the business in their head.
9. The Victory of ...a business that does not hang on you and pull you down. (Can't stop thinking about what needs to be done or what didn't get done).
10. The Victory of ...a business and a life that you enjoy because you are doing what you do with intention and purpose, because it's the work and the life you actually love and desire.

Yes, your business can be orderly and predictable – and rewarding. It is my desire to show you the systems development process as the narrow road to this kind of a business with a fruitful life, not a job. The journey begins by creating order.

CHAPTER 2

Systems Create Order from Chaos

Becoming the Intelligent Designer of your business

"It is best to do things systematically, since we are only human and disorder is our worst enemy."

— Hesiod

You've heard the outburst before; someone is at their wits end with the work they're doing (or redoing) or they're irritated trying to find a tool or supplies to complete a job and in utter frustration they blurt out, "dang it, we need a system for _____ (you fill in the blank)." My outburst came one night standing in our kitchen, looking for the popcorn.

We all felt it: my wife, my daughter, and me. Our home kitchen pantry was out of control and a source of constant frustration. It wouldn't have been so bad if it was a random closet that we accessed once a year to get Christmas decorations - but this was the central walk-in closet that housed not just food but pots and pans, the dog food, and many other frequently used kitchen items.

It wasn't life and death stuff, but just the dumb frustration of searching for something that you needed at that moment and couldn't find or access. The shelves of food concealed what was behind them and so the search for a can of tuna was a five minute ordeal. The floor was cluttered with stuff from our last party so it was nearly impossible to walk into the "walk-in" closet.

What was lacking was order. So I was on a mission, a systematization mission. The next free Saturday I created...*The Ultimate Kitchen Pantry System* (careful that's trademarked.)

The details of how to do this type of systemization will be revealed later but suffice it to say, it was not a patch job or a bandage. *Disorganization is often the first step to systemization*, so I completely emptied the pantry of everything inside, which made the rest of the house look like a wreck. The pantry re-do system included a trip to Home Depot for materials for custom shelves, an assortment of bins, and all the needed hardware. The shelves and bins were designed according to specific areas for each item and more importantly a re-evaluation of everything in the kitchen pantry. After all, why have something close at hand that's only used once a year?

An important detail of systemization is labels, so that **"everyone knows where everything goes."** My favorite quote on this subject is, "organization is not systemization." You know from experience that just because you "organized" the garage once it didn't stay that way. Now you know why. Unless everyone knows how to use the system and knows where

> **"Everyone knows where everything goes."**

everything belongs, the organization quickly deteriorates.

So how does my weekend kitchen project apply to your business? My point in telling you my kitchen pantry makeover story is that we've all experienced the need for systems in every area of our lives. We know how to clean up and organize a closet or our car or the kids' toys, but what's missing is the intentionality to create a system. Now you may think this is crazy, but it's why your work of organizing an area hasn't stuck: *the system for using and enforcing the system is incomplete (see Chapter 11, Making Your Systems Stick).*

Not only have we experienced the need for systems in each area of our lives to create order, but if we've seen or experienced order anywhere it is because of a system. That is huge! Let me say it again…If we have seen or experienced order, it is because of a system.

Order is the evidence of effective systemization. Said another way, order is the sign of intelligent design. There's not a better way to describe the systemization process than intelligent design.

As applied to business development - when you see an orderly business, you know there is a business owner, who is an intelligent designer, creative, and an innovator who has very intentional wisdom and knows the idea of how that business should serve its customers.

Hard-core evolutionists want us to believe that randomness and time created something orderly. If you own a business you know that's impossible – no, wait, if you own a garage you know it's impossible. That's exactly why you need a system for everything, everything, everything - because without a systems approach things fall apart and disorder reigns.

Our goal is to create an orderly business...a business that is predictable and efficient while it serves its clients and customers in a memorable way. Order is the goal, but it's not the end game. We don't want order because it looks nice, we want order because it's the narrow path that leads to profits. One of the reasons systems create order and order creates profits is because labor is the biggest number on almost every business' P and L. Work of any kind that's done in a haphazard, slapdash fashion takes longer and usually has to be redone, causing the bottom line labor costs to suffer.

The quote at the beginning of this chapter is also posted in the pole-barn at Interior Plant Scapes. The pole-barn is our main work area for prepping plants and planters for new installations and potting hundreds of plants every couple of weeks; it's an enormous amount of work activity in a small area. The sign on the wall reads:

It is best to do things systematically, since we are only human and disorder is our worst enemy.

That was not written by me; it was not written by some business guru, or any other smart business consultant. It was not written in the last hundred years, no not even the last thousand years.

It was written by Hesiod, a Greek poet and thought leader of his time, 650 BC. If Hesiod knew 2,500 years ago that "disorder is our greatest enemy" – I'm thinking he must've had a garage!

If you're a small business owner, can you think of a quote more appropriate for your day-to-day life? It is best to do things systematically, since we are only human, and disorder is our worst enemy. Let me assure you, disorder is the enemy of anything and everything you're trying to accomplish. Disorder is the enemy of your staff development, your personal development, your time management, your sales goals, and of course, your life apart from your business.

Use this as a daily reminder in the systemization quest for your business and life: disorder is your worst enemy. Again, that's why if you see order of any kind there was a designer responsible for the order, and it's how you must think of yourself – The Designer and Architect of Orderly Systems for the _____ Business (fill-in-the-blank with the name of your business).

Let me repeat that, if orderliness is the sign of Intelligent Design then that is the name you want to call yourself and I want you to get excited about the possibilities. "I am the Intelligent Designer of my business. I am the Designer, the Innovator, the Inventor, and the Creator of my small business that operates with precision, excellence, impeccable order, and intention."

What is a System?

So if systemization is the path to order, what exactly is a system? More importantly, how do you create them? Let's start with a good working definition:

A system is a method or set of principles by which something is organized or by which a process is executed.

Think about that definition in the most basic and fundamental terms possible. I mean really simplify the idea of systems in your own thinking. Leonardo DaVinci, a supreme intelligent designer, said, "Simplicity is the ultimate sophistication."

Likewise your best business systems will be the simplest ones.

So don't think too lofty, like systemization is some new concept you have to learn. You are already very familiar with systems and you use them regularly every day. We live with and *in* systems, and in fact we *are* systems.

Your human body is the perfect example of an integration of systems that work together in harmony for a common goal and purpose: sustaining your life! The circulatory system of blood flow enables the respiratory system of oxygenation, which enables the muscular systems, which is dependent on the skeletal system which....you get the idea.

Look around you for other examples of superior simple systems that could be used or adapted to your business operation.

1. Fill in the blank forms – these are templates that don't require instruction and yet get the desired information.

2. Paint by number sets – put the color red in every section with a #1, yellow in the sections with #4, etc., paint within the lines and viola, you have a finished work very close to the original.

3. Recipes – if you use this combination of ingredients, in these amounts, and prepare them in this manner, you will get the same results again and again.

4. Computers – the software in a computer is a system of algorithms arranged so that the input creates the desired output.

5. Language – letters in the right order create words, words in the right order create sentences, and sentences in the right order create ideas.

So again, a system is...a method or set of principles by which something is organized or by which a process is executed.

As you begin the systems development process for your business (or your personal life), it's essential to get your arms around everything that can possibly be used to create *"the methods by which your work is organized and your processes executed."*

> **A system is...a method or set of principles by which something is organized or by which a process is executed.**

Think about how you can use these other examples of systems:

1. Step-by-step instructions
2. Step-by-step diagrams
3. Step-by-step photos
4. Before and after photos
5. Photos of right way and wrong way
6. Measuring cups and devices
7. Step-by-step recipes
8. Forms with instructions for work to be done
9. Templates – fill in the blank
10. Design packages
11. Bundled packages of any kind
12. Sample of the finished product
13. Drop down lists of options
14. Opening duties and closing duties
15. Scripts and memorization work

16. Scripted sales presentations
17. Scripted telephone answering
18. Training manuals
19. Checklists for completion
20. Checklists for loading materials
21. Jigs or guides for manufacturing
22. FAQ guides (frequently asked questions)
23. Service schedules and route work
24. Time In and Time Out Form (to track billable time)

Use this list not just for your own business, but to learn to identify systems in other businesses that could possibly be adapted to yours.

Listen, I want you to become Systems Obsessed! I want you to fight for order and systems in every detail of your business. I want you to be a student of systems: business systems, nature and eco-systems, the solar system, you name it. Become a student of order. When you see order, try to describe and document the system behind the order.

You need some inspiration for the benefits you're going to derive from the systemization process for your business. So go looking for order, and then look for the design and the designer's intent behind the order.

Go Looking For Order

Here's your first assignment: take a trip to McDonald's. Don't worry, you don't have to eat the food if you don't want to, just order a cup of coffee and sit down with a legal pad and describe the systems you observe.

First of all, you probably won't have to travel far from your home or business to find one! There's probably a McDonald's less than five miles away. Why? Because someone designed it that way. McDonald's corporate office has demographic systems to know exactly how many people need to live in a certain area to support a restaurant and how far one McDonald's should be from another.

Go inside and study McDonald's system orchestration as if you're going to write a 100-page report on it. You don't even have to go behind the scenes to see the food prep systems to study the order. No, just stand out front and pretend like you're not sure what to order and observe all the systems:

- No one needs to be handed a menu at this restaurant because they're posted on the wall (an innovation).
- The menu is posted in the same place at every McDonald's, above the order takers (an innovation).
- You can order fast by package plan and by number, "give me a #1 with a Coke" (an innovation).

Then your meal is prepared by hundreds of small and incremental system innovations:

- The ice for your drink is added to the line on the cup.
- The "large size" drink button on the soda machine is pushed to fill to the brim with no one watching.
- Your hamburger is cooked on a grill with two temperature settings: on and off, simplicity in it's finest.
- The ketchup and mustard are applied with a gun in the exact

amount, with one squeeze of the trigger.

- Your fries are automatically lowered into the oil and automatically lifted when they're done.

The best way to study McDonald's is to go to three different locations all in the same day. Spend an hour in each and study what's the same and what's different. The operation is exactly the same, the décor may be different. Diverse decors are an innovation. In an effort to create a connection with «your» McDonald›s, each restaurant could have a décor theme. The Everblades hockey team in our town (SW Florida, close to the Everglades) has quite a following and I saw a McDonald's with an Everblades-themed décor. So here is an example of an element in a McDonald›s franchise that can be different and yet, do no harm to the business system; instead actually helps it.

But what's most instructive to study in McDonald's or any business is the sameness. What are the processes they've created that deliver the same consistent results repeatedly? Systems are useless if they cannot be duplicated.

The Success is in the System

If you can't replicate the process, you can't duplicate the success. That is a million dollar sentence! It is the Holy Grail for your business development. You must learn how to replicate the processes that drive the core deliverables of your business. Not just the order fulfillment of the product or service you sell, but the selling and the marketing of it as well. If you can't replicate the lead generation (the marketing) - and you can't replicate the lead conversion (the selling), then sadly you don't have a viable business. The economic meltdown that was blamed for the demise of hundreds of small businesses was not the culprit; it was the inability of the owners to create systems to drive customers to their door, eager to do business with them. Yes, you can replicate the process of sales and marketing.

Back to our McDonald's field trip and systems recon mission. As you go to three different Mickey D's, obviously the food is exactly the same and so is the menu and where it's located, but what's instructive is the operation of the systems. The whole thing works in the hands of people who have been trained to operate the system to deliver a constant result: consistently ordinary food.

To be more exact, McDonald's systems operate in the hands of teenagers. Systems are a beautiful thing, yes, but never more beautiful and more productive than when they're working well in the hands of someone else. That's my goal and the purpose of this book.

That is replicating the process and that's what McDonald's has masterfully created: a franchise prototype, business model with systems that are integrated to give their customers exactly what they want. What do their customers want? No, they don't want gourmet food, but they want the same exact experience of food every time they go, regardless of which McDonald's they visit. That's called control. That's what your customers want too...control! **They want the same consistent, reliable results and the same experience every time they choose to do business with you.**

The customer wants the control and the ability to duplicate their experience with your business any time they want.

You can't duplicate the success if you can't replicate the process

That can't happen without systems. ***You can't duplicate the success if you can't replicate the process.***

Your business success and your customer's experience will be hit or miss without systems. The order we are striving to create is not order for order's sake, it's order because we want a successful and profitable business.

Let's be very clear about the amount of benefits you're going to enjoy by investing in the systems development process. In the next chapter you're not only going to be told about the systems development process...you're going to be sold. You must be absolutely convinced and therefore, obsessed with the work of systems creation and innovation in your business. You'll need a vision big enough and exciting enough to see you through. The benefits are real, the lifestyle is doable, and most of all, the profits are attainable. Basically the bottom line is systems will increase your bottom line – you will make more money!

Whatever motivates and excites you the most -- peace of mind, lifestyle options, or more profits - the benefits and rewards from the implementation of systems development are there.

CHAPTER 3

Fall In Love with Systems

17 Beautiful Benefits of Systems

"The Success is in the System."

— **AT&T**

Most people knew Zig Ziglar as a motivational speaker, but he got his start as a sales trainer. Zig was consistently in the top one or two of hundreds of salesman in the cookware company he worked for. Zig knew how to sell. One of my favorite Zig stories about how to close a sale emphasized the fact that customers don't buy because they see your small amount of value (the benefits of your product) next to their big pile of money. His point was that you as the salesperson must create a very significant measure of value and benefits of what your product does, so that it towers over the prospect's sum of money.

I want you to invest in your business and your future lifestyle. I want you to invest in the systems development process. Therefore, I'm going to create a large amount of value and benefits so that you'll stay the course and get it done.

1. ***Systems create order and stability.*** If systems create order, then order creates stability and stability in a business is a beautiful thing. An orderly and stable business means that everyone knows what's expected of them and they have the tools and training to do their work well. Order and stability means the business owner knows who they are and who their best customers are, which results in a steady stream of income which pays the bills and makes payroll each week.

2. ***Systems require less-skilled labor.*** One of the goals of your systems is to "leverage ordinary employees with extraordinary systems." The point is, there are very few extraordinary people, and if your business depends on superstars for every position then your business is not duplicable. Great businesses, however, have been built with mostly ordinary people who've been empowered and enabled to do amazing things.

3. ***Systems reduce labor costs.*** Less-skilled labor costs less. Most small business franchise operations (system driven businesses) rely heavily on entry level positions that are paid a lower wage. These jobs are a great training ground to learn and gain confidence. They work because someone has innovated the process (the nuts and bolts tasks) so that an unskilled person who is properly trained can get great results. Personally I hire the very best attitude and then teach them my Plant Care system to become a Green Thumb is less than four weeks. They are my front-line Business Representatives.

4. ***Systems hire Attitude over Ability.*** It takes a while to learn that what you think is a great employee is not necessarily so. Every once in a while we'll get an applicant that has years of experience in our industry and they look like a homerun. Our hiring

system, however, has numerous ways to reveal what matters most: *nice people who love life and other people.* Those are the people that create business success and do amazing things. As I mentioned before, I can teach plants and plant care because I have innovated that training system for years. The project you don't want as a business owner is trying to fix a bad attitude, no matter how good they are at what they do.

> **Hire the very best attitude – then teach them to get amazing results with your systems.**

5. <u>**Systems make training predictable and measurable**</u>. Also related to the above-mentioned benefit, a systematic approach to learning the ins and outs of any job function makes training easier and straightforward. Most service and quality problems in business can be traced back to a sloppy, haphazard approach to training. Conversely, when you experience mannered professional people who serve you with excellence, you're witnessing the result of a systemized training program. On this, I speak with experience: hiring the best candidate, but not investing the time and effort into their training – only to have it come back again and again and create problems.

6. <u>**Systems create employee confidence**</u>. When you're not good at what you do, it's no fun and you get easily discouraged and give up. But, make me look like a superstar and teach me to serve people in meaningful ways and you have my loyalty for years. The Starbucks Barista training program takes raw recruits (with great attitudes who love people) and teaches them to create drinks people love and pay big bucks for. Many Barista's blossom with the new found confidence and become store managers and

career employees.

7. **_Systems increase capacity_**. Your business can serve more people faster when it works systematically. You can innovate most job functions so that the task just takes less time to do. Innovation eliminates wasted steps. Sometimes it's a tool or piece of equipment that increases capacity and other times it is a complete reengineering of a work process – or it could be both. From using a Sub-Irrigation system (an innovation) for our individual plants so they need water less often and scanning a bar-code in and out of each account (equipment) - to scripting all the steps of an account visit from parking to getting water (process) we have nearly doubled our capacity from once-a-week visits to once every two weeks. Can you say "Huge?"

8. **_Systems eliminate (most) dumb mistakes_**. Because systems create a repetitive approach to the simplest tasks, they become second nature. The dumb mistakes are the result of having to rethink and make up the "policy du-jour." If your business is plagued by constant product defects or silly service issues, you're dying the slow painful death of a thousand cuts.

9. **_Systems create predictability_.** In business, being predictable is a good thing. Predictability is what drives the stock market and it's what people invest in. Having a methodical and tried and true approach to your business gives customers confidence.

10. **_Systems give people control_**. Similar to predictability, control is the ability to recreate a customer experience over and over again. Yes, your systems give you and your employees control over the business operation, but even more importantly, systems **_give your customers control_** over their experience! If I'm

the customer and I can replicate my experience with your business anytime I want, I have control. Hence, the popularity of chain restaurants. People are most picky about their food and a franchise prototype restaurant like Bonefish Grill assures me that when I'm hankering for the Bang-Bang Shrimp all I have to do is call and order it, or go in, sit down, and viola.

11. **_Systems create a steady stream of new prospects_**. Prospecting in a business is marketing – gaining the attention and interest of people who have the ability to do business with you. Marketing is also called lead-generation. If you don't have a systematic and reliable method for generating leads, your business is vulnerable to say the least. A lead-generation system can be automated to work like a water faucet and create a steady stream of qualified prospects eager to learn more about your business. The faucet can be turned on full or turned down to a trickle depending on your ability to follow up and fulfill.

> **If you don't have a systematic and reliable method for generating leads, your business is vulnerable.**

12. **_Systems create a profile to pursue your best prospect._** Not all business is good business, which means not all prospects are worth the pursuit. The starting point of creating marketing systems is knowing exactly who is your best prospect and why. The marketing system will establish categories of prospects by industry and create hot buttons (or reasons I want to buy) for each type. *"You can't sell John Smith what John Smith buys, until you see the world through John Smith's eyes."* This means you'll have a system for not only identifying who is your best prospect, but more importantly, why they are and why they buy.

13. *Systems create a steady stream of new customers.* A prospect is not a customer. Lead generation systems create the opportunity, but lead conversion systems create (convert) customers. There's no such thing as a born salesman, because the skills of a professional salesperson are in fact systems that can be learned and skills that can be honed. Bad salespeople think all they need is the gift of gab. Professionals invest the time to learn the skills and scripts so they're perceived as consultants and problem solvers. Successful selling is a disciplined approach to learning and executing the selling systems.

14. *Systems balance the new sales versus order fulfillment pipelines.* This is the hardest balance to maintain for most small business owners – not out-selling your company's ability to deliver the goods. Every business needs trained staff that can meet the demands of new sales – but not too many staff, and not too many sales too fast. That's called making your business scalable.

15. *Systems make your business scalable.* New sales and marketing systems can be controlled like a water faucet. Turn it on full when the market is dry and you need new customers, or dial it back a notch when your team is at or near capacity. When sales consistently outpace order fulfillment, systems are also the best and fastest way to get new hires up to speed to deliver the goods with excellence and predictability.

16. *Systems create more profit.* All of the above together create a profitable business. When you can do the work of your business with less labor and fewer defects you can create profit. Of course your margins have to make sense, meaning you must be charging enough, but if you're under the pressure of price constraints because of a competitive market, you're only other choice is

to do business better. "Innovate (systemize) or die." Premium prices are a wonderful thing, but when combined with process equity (innovative and proprietary methods) and great systems you have the ultimate money machine.

17. **_Systems give the business owner autonomy and freedom._** This is the reward for all your hard work, and as I've already mentioned it is a sweet reward and worth the effort. The ability to create a business that works without you there is the ultimate vocational pursuit. If you'll commit to the systems development process and keep these other benefits before you, you can enjoy this ultimate reward and lifestyle.

> **Systems create a business that "works" – without you.**

Let's get started then to make these beautiful benefits a reality in your business.

CHAPTER 4

Micro-Manage Your Business ... to the Max

Systems designed to create a business that works...without you

"Delegation without Systemization is Frustration."

- Brad Miller

Whether it's the "get the kids ready for school system," the "grocery shopping system," or the ultimate car organization system, the systems development process will create order in every area of your life. You'll have a new freedom in your personal surroundings and even in your thinking as you apply a systems approach to the key areas of your life. You may think I'm exaggerating but my kitchen pantry still gives me a sense of joy and order when life is a bit chaotic.

Our goal now though, is to apply the systems development process to our businesses and more specifically to create systems so that our business can operate in the capable hands of our staff.

Do you want to know why it's so hard to entrust the work of your business to others and why the principal frustrations are with staff just not getting it right? Micheal Gerber makes an excellent point in *The E-Myth* about delegation. To analyze why most business people have difficulty hiring and entrusting the work of the business to employees, he correctly diagnoses the problem as abdication instead of delegation. Let me explain the difference.

Delegation is the orderly and systematic transfer of an area of responsibility in the business to another person – a staff member. Delegation that's complete and effective includes documentation of the task (procedure manual or pictures or videos, etc.) accompanied with step-by-step and side-by-side training. But that's not the way it usually happens. Abdication is more the norm. Abdication is the renouncing, stepping down, and giving up of responsibility. Picture someone who is frustrated and in defeat, brushing off their hands and walking away.

The small business owner who's at his wit's end, over-worked and over-whelmed is the one who abdicates crucial areas of the business. They may think they have delegated the responsibilities but, *delegation without systemization is frustration*.

The story is the same in most small businesses because there are a lot of moving parts to make a business work. The business owner has most of this knowledge in his or her own head, especially if it's a start-up and just in the process of hiring the first employees. The knowledge of how to do the business with its myriad of nuances is collective and familiar to the business owner and *he or she wrongly assumes that other people naturally know what to do.* That's the fatal flaw in businesses, large and small, assuming that a new hire (or even a long-term hire) knows what to do and how to do it and… is actually doing it.

Without the aid of a procedural manual that has systematically chronicled all the information out of the business owner's head so that it is available for others, their only choice is to abdicate and walk away.

Yes, delegation without systemization is frustration. It's frustration to the employee who's left to figure it out, it's frustration to customers who don't get a consistent and predictable experience with your company, and it's extra frustration for you because employees left to their own devices create *policy du jour*.

It's time to take a different approach and have an absolute bias towards systems. We will apply a systems mentality to all areas of your company, and then entrust these areas into the hands of others. Our business will operate smoothly in the capable hands of others. Before you entrust your business to others, you must first give them clear and exact instructions on how everything works. By everything, I mean literally everything.

Warning: I'm about to make a statement that will rock your world and most likely your basic belief systems about business. **"You must learn to micro-manage every detail of your business."** Are you still with me? This is a term that has only negative connotations associated with it. The employee says, "Stop micro-managing me," or the business owner has to know the employee's every move and routinely takes back tasks because "I can do it better myself." Certainly there's some micro-managing that's unproductive but what if the micro-managing is not from a person looking over your shoulder?

In our new systemization bias, micro-managing is not a bad thing – it's a good thing, an essential and freeing thing! Listen, you must micro-manage every detail of your entire business operation.

And here's the goal: **You must micro-manage the systems creation process – so that you don't have to micro-manage your people.** Once you've created the systems in precise detail, your people are free to operate the systems, and you're free to do anything else you'd like to do. You are now a business owner.

> **You must micro-manage the systems creation process – so that you don't have to micro-manage your people.**

If you're the inventor and the creator then you are going to micro-manage every detail of how you want your business to look, feel, and operate. You're the one responsible for the remarkable and unique customer experience that differentiates your business. Nothing can be to be left to chance and nothing can be left to employee discretion, whim, or preference. The business you are creating does what it does with absolute intention and purpose so that it delivers the same predicable and stellar experience every single time. That can only happen when you micro-manage the systems development process in every aspect of your business.

You, the business owner, must decide how you want your telephone answered...exactly, precisely, scripted, and memorized by your staff. You, the business owner, must decide what you want your staff to look like, exactly what you want them to wear and their personal grooming. You, the business owner, must decide upon hundreds of minute details of explicitly how the business will run in the hands of others. You must micro-manage the systems development process of your business. Then and only then does your staff have the ability to do the work that's satisfying to them and serves your clients with excellence, and then and only then can you say you have a real business and not a job.

This micro-managing process can be thought of as scripting the entire customer experience from beginning to end. Later, I'll tell you the story of a doctor who wanted his patients to experience health care in a new way. He thought through the whole process and micro-managed every little detail imagining that he was the patient.

Obviously, this is a huge task when you consider all the elements of your business, so let's break down the systems into three large categories. Every one of your systems will fall into one of these three areas:

1. Order Fulfillment

When the prospect has said, "Yes, I'll take it," you must deliver the goods. Systems are critical to the delivery of your goods and services with excellence and consistency. This is your opportunity to innovate and differentiate the customer experience so that people are happy, talking to others, and coming back repeatedly.

2. Sales and Marketing

Marketing is lead generation and sales is lead conversion. The type of business you have will determine your sales and marketing methods, but bottom line is you need both and they need to be systemized.

3. Management and Measurement

If you want anything to improve, it must be measured. There's no way to know if you're winning if you don't keep score. Far from being a boring exercise that you dread, management and measuring systems can get you (and your staff) pumped and excited about your business. You'll celebrate successes like never before because you have real life data that shows you're making progress.

CHAPTER 5

Recipes for Success

Systemizing the Order Fulfillment Process

"If you can't measure it, you can't manage it."

- **Peter Drucker**

During the first year of starting my business I was a waiter at a fine dining restaurant in Fort Myers. This was actually my second stint, as I had worked there a couple of years before but left to start my catering business (see the introduction if you missed that story). Now I was back to make some money to pay the bills while the business got on its feet (the key roadblock that small business people must get past during a start-up: bringing home the bacon until the business has paying customers).

One night a woman asked me, "Who's your chef?" This after having a few bites of her Veal entrée and obviously impressed with the presentation and quality of the food.

I'll never forget the answer I gave; I'll never forget it because it was incredibly stupid. "Oh, he's a local kid."

It was a ridiculous and classless answer because it didn't do anything to posture me, the waiter, or the restaurant as upscale and elite. What I could have said was, "I'm not certain where he received his formal training, but he's a top professional."

She associated the great results, her delicious food, with a master chef that had been educated and trained in Paris or New York City or a top culinary school. The person responsible for her delicious dinner *was* a local kid! It was Kelly, and I'd known him for years and he was a good line cook, but not yet a professional chef. How was it then that the restaurant's "order fulfillment system" of quality entrees served at premium prices be consistently delivered by Kelly, the local kid?

The reality is, it was the recipes – and recipes are systems. There was a large three-ring binder in the kitchen office and it had the recipe for everything...even down to the condiments and hand-made salad dressings. Today, almost 30 years later, the restaurant is still a Fort Myers staple, known for an intimate dining experience and consistently great food. All done in the hands of trained staff, not the owner.

Recipes Are Systems

The plants at this restaurant are amazing too. I know because my wife and I eat dinner there quite often and I get to see my company's work firsthand.

For the best and most successful restaurants, the food preparation processes are not in the chef's head, they are written down, documented and then rigidly followed. Again, they're called recipes.

A recipe is a food prep system. To duplicate the success, you replicate the process - and that's exactly what recipes do. Think of even the most basic recipe for baking cookies. You have a list of ingredients, and you use those ingredients and only those.

A list of ingredients is a system. You have a measured amount of each of those ingredients, and you use the amount specified, no less and no more. Measuring cups and spoons are systems. Scales to measure weight and volume are systems.

You have a process for how the ingredients are designed to come together. There is an order to how they're added, when they're added, and how long they have to cook. Depending on where you got the recipe, there may even be a picture of the finished product. Pictures are a system tool that should be used wherever possible. A detailed list of instructions is a system.

The system that was responsible for that woman's meal that night was an order fulfillment system. The core deliverables for the restaurant are great food and great service. These are what the customers of the restaurant willingly trade for money. The core deliverables are the products and/or services that a business provides to its customers and it must provide them in a predictable and consistent manner every time.

If a business is hit or miss, sometimes good and sometimes bad, the buying public promptly figures that out and knows they don't have control over their buying experience. If that's the case, they take their business someplace else where they do have control.

Order fulfillment systems assure the business owner that the customer will get the same precise experience every time they want to buy what that business sells, whether it's a restaurant or a plumbing service.

As I pointed out in the McDonald's restaurant example, it doesn't have to be a Five Star culinary dining experience. It can be an average experience – as long as the experience is consistent and predictable.

Now compare the previous restaurant scenario to one of my favorite Food Network shows: *Diners, Drive-Ins and Dives*, with host Guy Fietti. He visits and spars with the cooks of small, out-of-the-way "joints" that have a funky atmosphere and great food. Very often the food is prepared by the owner or by one person who has the magic in their head. Fietti cooks side by side with these talented people as they blend their love for food with the food prep techniques of a pinch of that and a handful of this.

> **Get the business (the order fulfillment system) out of your head!**

These people typically work twelve hour days whenever the restaurant is open because, and here's the lesson...the order fulfillment system isn't written down. No one else knows how to get the same results because the owner or chef hasn't invested the time to document and train anyone else on the order fulfillment system.

Or, as is very often the case, this key employee knows the job security of having the system in his head, "They can't fire me, no-one else knows how to make this stuff."

The only thing worse than having all your business order fulfillment systems in your own head, is having them in an employee's head. You may laugh (you should cry if it describes you) but it happens all the time. An employee knows they have job security because only they know how to do some of the vital functions of the business.

The core promise of my company, Interior Plant Scapes, is "Plants and Planters Guaranteed Gorgeous," therefore, our essential order fulfillment systems are built around the promise of gorgeous plants.

It's amazing how some of our competitors don't understand that. An ugly plant in an otherwise professional building, (hotel, office or the like) is like blood in the water to our sales team.

We'll talk about sales and marketing systems in just a bit, but we have a multistep campaign message built around the inability of our competition (or a DIY business owner) to deliver the core promise of our industry – gorgeous plants.

Order Fulfillment Systems

The order fulfillment of delivering and guaranteeing gorgeous plants is so crucial to our success that we have dozens of systems built around that promise.

Let me explain the nuts and bolts of our order fulfillment systems.

I've intentionally included a lot of detail of this core deliverable of our business, not so you can start a plant leasing company, but so you can see the detail and transferable ideas for your own order fulfillment systems. See my list after each of the systems I describe.

Guaranteed, gorgeous plants start with the plants we buy.

The Plant Purchasing System

We buy foliage plants from fewer than ten growers, mostly in Florida, and each grower is on our Master Plant Chart. The Master

Plant Chart includes years of innovation about exactly which plants we use, the pot size we buy them in, the pot size they're up-potted to, where the plant is located in our greenhouses, etc. Also, the chart includes the first choice, second choice and third choice providers of the plant we need. Through years of trial and error we know who grows the best of each variety we use. If they're out we go to the next on the list.

Transferable Systems and Innovations:

1. Purchasing system – a detailed list of every ingredient, tool, supply, parts list, etc., that you need to fulfill an order. Not just to buy right, but more importantly to save the expense of going back to complete a job because someone forgot to order a $2.00 part. Not to mention the hassle to the customer because their job/installation was not completed on time as promised.

2. Vendor systems – not just exactly what you buy, but who is the best vendor for everything you buy. Not just in price, but customer service, quality, terms, and their own predictable systems that make doing business with them easy and smooth.

3. Quick reference chart or notebook – an efficient system of every tool and supply you use for order fulfilment in one place. If you'll invest the time and effort to do this once, the time you'll save in your purchasing process will reap rewards (saved labor hours) for years to come.

The Tremendous 25 Plant System

When I started my company I had this wild idea that the more variety in plant material was best – Wrong! Our plant palette of the plants we use is now precise and intentional to the extreme. This has to be a firm decision we are committed to or else the growers and their "specials list" will determine our plant designs. Again, through trial and lots of error we've narrowed our plant inventory to the top performing foliage. Remember our goal and promise is Guaranteed Gorgeous plants, so we don't put just any plant on an account – it must be tested and proven. It must be one of the Tremendous 25.

Our industry peers think wild designs with lots of plant variety is important; we've learned our customers want gorgeous, clean and fresh plants, period! Our industry peers want to win industry best design awards...we want longterm customer retention and hugely profitable accounts.

Transferable Systems and Innovations:

1. Consistent and predictable systems – what are you absolutely sure that you can deliver every time, on time, with excellence? Don't even think of expanding your line and product offerings until you have your core deliverables systemized to perfection.

2. Narrow product offerings - Don't try to be all things to all people because not all business is good business or profitable business. The hardest thing for a business owner to say is "No, I'm sorry we don't offer that." Become known for doing a few things exceptionally well; the few things you can build solid systems around. We often jokingly say to prospects, "if you need a shovel, you've got the wrong guys. All we do is plants and planters. To be precise, Plants and Planters Guaranteed Gorgeous." We don't do landscaping or lawn care.

3. Industry Contrarian – Beware of your industry norms, you

don't want to be an industry norm. Your business is driven by your best customer and best product for that customer, not what industry peers do. The advertising industry is driven less by what the customer wants (sales) and more by the quest for CLIO awards. There may be some prospects in our market that want elaborate designs and lots of plant variety (not many I assure you) but that's not our best customer. Regis McKenna, a highly praised marketing consultant says, "many companies fail to realize that *which* companies they attract is often more important than how many they attract."

4. Standardization is usually more profitable than customization. Customization is hard to build systems around and even harder to charge enough to make it profitable, as is the case with standardization.

The Plant Replacement Form (reminder: forms are powerful systems)

Here's a little secret of the professional plant care business: it's sometimes less about horticultural expertise and more about replacing an ugly plant with a new gorgeous one. Since we routinely replace numerous plants every week, dispersed everywhere inside offices and resorts, at hundreds of locations across three counties, we need a form that accomplishes a lot. Our Plant Replacement Form is constantly being tweaked to make it more accurate and effective. It is the primary communication tool from the field technicians (gardeners) to the delivery & installation department to complete a needed plant replacement. This is a fundamental form to keeping our promise of Plants and Planters Guaranteed Gorgeous. There's nothing more frustrating and costly than prepping, loading, and delivering a replacement plant, only to show up and find it's the wrong size or type of plant. Aaarrrgghh! That never happens to us anymore though. (And if you believe that, I have some awesome property just south of us in the Everglades I'd love to sell you.)

Transferable Systems and Innovations:

1. Inner office forms to facilitate order fulfillment are some of the most essential ingredients of your business development plan; invest lots of time to get them just right. Use your service blunders and mistakes to assess your forms to see what went wrong and if an improved form can fix it.

2. Passing the Baton – Make sure that your systems are fully integrated so that as one department passes the order fulfillment work to the next, no one drops the baton in the pass. If your business has field techs, you need a stellar system for how the work orders they create get into the office to be fulfilled. Surprisingly, I found most service errors and customer call-ins (complaints) happened not because the paperwork wasn't done but because the form didn't make it to the next department.

The Delivery and Installation System

Now that you know our secret for gorgeous plants (lots of plant replacements), I have to tell you about the system for installing the plants into the planters, what we call decorative containers. This is nuts and bolts innovation for a process that is repeated several times a week, often in the middle of a gorgeous hotel lobby or the office of the CEO. Since we are dealing with soil, water, and our moss covering the pots, the process must be efficient, neat, and orchestrated with precision. To systemize the plant replacement process of "in with the new and out with the old" we have custom made carts, tools, and procedures that we have perfected over the years. The delivery and installation of plant replacements also includes systems for loading and unloading, so plants don't get crushed, along with routing systems to map out the stops for maximum efficiency.

Transferable Systems and Innovations:

1. Process Equity – Your innovations in your order fulfillment systems are what will differentiate your business from all of your competitors. The term process equity means that when you have innovated, tweaked, invented, and designed something your business does with beauty and elegance, you truly have an asset. Extreme profitability in the process is also essential if you want to really call it an asset. Here is a great question to ask yourself: "For what opportunity do my talents, experience, and ability give me a unique advantage in the marketplace?" If you can't think of any, then your job is to create and maintain an advantage. You can't do business on a level playing field, you need unique process equity. As one of my business mentors said, "I want to shoot fish in a barrel; and I want it to be a small barrel with no water and a really big fish, and I want a bazooka!"

2. Custom Tools and Equipment – If the process is something that's repetitive and time consuming, the investment in custom equipment will pay off in no time. Because the biggest job we do every day is bringing water to potted plants inside buildings, we have custom watering machines that hold up to 18 gallons of water and roll right up to the plants. Imagine carrying that much water around in watering cans every day. The best way to revolutionize and create custom equip-

ment is to work "in" the order fulfillment as an employee doing the work, but with the mindset of an inventor working "on" it to create and improve the process.

3. Step by Step Process – To really wrap your mind around the whole order fulfillment process, think about all the steps from the signed agreement/contract to a happy and satisfied customer. The steps are most likely small systems that can be identified and innovated, so that when you are done, your order fulfillment is a collection of integrated systems. Think of the steps involved in making a pot of coffee, or making a peanut butter and jelly sandwich. Step-by-step is breaking the process down into small, incremental parts that can be described, documented, and easily transferred as a training module.

One of the main struggles most small businesses have is balancing the sales and marketing of their services with the order fulfillment of the product that was just sold. Once you create the sales and marketing systems we talk about in the next chapter, you want to have the confidence that your order fulfillment can keep up. Your investment in documenting and updating every little detail of how you serve customers with the thing you do, whether it's fixing their plumbing or fixing their hair, will allow you to keep the sales and marketing systems going full force.

CHAPTER 6

Random Acts of Marketing VS Marketing Systems

Systemizing the Lead Generation Process

> *"If you can't create a system that brings you a sufficient quantity and quality of leads on a continual and steady basis, you can't control your business."*
>
> **- Dan Kennedy**

Maybe when you read that quote from Dan Kennedy, you're thinking, "is that even possible?" If you're wondering if this whole systems creation stuff can be applied to marketing – you're going to love this chapter. Yes, you can create systems that bring you, "a sufficient quantity and quality of leads on a continual basis," and so therefore, yes, you can have the ultimate control of your business!

Your marketing can be systemized. Your selling can by systemized. Which means, you can have a predictable stream of customers and cash flow. Once you create marketing systems you can also expect:

- A clear picture of your ideal prospect, perfectly matched for your business.
- Prospects that come to you pre-qualified and predisposed to doing business with you.
- An end to cold call selling, but an endless stream of warm-call opportunities.
- Referrals and testimonials that perpetuate your systems so that marketing and selling is automated.
- Automated marketing campaigns – "set it, and forget it."

That's the goal of this chapter, and believe me it's possible, but this is only an introduction into what should be a lifetime of study and passion if you're a business owner or manager. Nothing is more important than mastering sales and marketing systems because if you don't have customers, you don't have a business.

If you have a firm grasp on the last chapter about how to create Order Fulfillment systems, this chapter on Marketing systems will really connect the dots, because the two should be completely integrated. Another way to think about these two is, order fulfillment is your Inside Reality and marketing is your Outside Perception.

Inside Reality and Outside Perception

One of my favorite marketing guys is Rich Harshaw. He's not only a great teacher of marketing concepts but has a company (Monopolize Your Marketplace) that has systemized many of the small business marketing functions.

As we just discussed in the previous chapter, order fulfillment is not just about how you deliver your core products and services, it's also about how you've innovated and differentiated your business. Harshaw has a marketing concept called Inside Reality vs. Outside Perception that perfectly describes the relationship between your order fulfillment systems and your marketing. Every business has both of these and they're either good or bad.

Again, inside reality is equal to order fulfillment: it's the culmination of everything you do to deliver a superior customer experience. It not only includes the systems and processes to give your customers "knock your socks off" service and killer products; inside reality also includes the company DNA: your character, integrity, work ethic, and commitment to serve people. Therefore, as we've all experienced in real life as customers, a business can either have a good and positive inside reality or...not so much.

The outside perception is how well your business does marketing to tell the world about your amazing inside reality. If someone says that a business is, "the best kept secret in town," that is not a compliment to the outside perception – but it is to the inside reality. What that statement means is that the business delivers a great product or service – but, sadly, tragically even, no one knows about it!

Our goal as business owners is to have an awesome inside reality and an outside perception of marketing systems that effectively and continually tells our best prospects about it.

Harshaw rightly describes the huge disparity between most company's inside reality and their outside perception. For example, if you judged Wal-Mart only by the outside perception of their TV commercials full of smiling and helpful people everywhere, you'd believe that was the inside reality of their store experience.

Whenever I go to Wal-Mart, (out of reluctant necessity), the inside reality is you can't actually find anyone to help you, and if you do you're an interruption of their work, not the reason for it. To be fair, their other outside perception is low prices, and that's definitely an inside reality.

It's been my experience that most small businesses that have been around for some time have figured out how to take care of their customers (their order fulfillment is pretty good), but they struggle to draw a continuous stream of qualified prospects eager to do business with them - their marketing stinks! They mistakenly believed the old adage, "if you just build a better mouse-trap, people will flock to your door." It just ain't so! Their attention to good service but inattention to marketing, keeps their business alive, but just barely. You don't want to just scrape by, but instead, flourish!

Let me just pause here and say again, in as strong and passionate terms as possible, you need to become a marketing expert! A marketing professional, a student and a teacher of great marketing – a guru even. If you're a small business owner, marketing is not casual reading - for you, it's study material.

> **You must become a Marketing Expert!**
>
> **Fall in love with systems – especially marketing systems.**

My all-time favorite Peter Drucker quote on this exact subject is,

"Because of the nature of business, it has just two functions, and only two. Marketing and innovation. Marketing and innovation make money. Everything else is a cost."

Read that again, better yet, memorize it. Make your business better and market it better, everything else is a distraction, and in small business the list of distractions is endless. Make your business better to constantly improve your inside reality – but even more important, make your marketing stellar so that your outside perception draws a continuous stream of qualified prospects eager to do business with you.

Dan Kennedy, who I referenced at the beginning of this chapter, urges business owners to stop thinking of themselves in the business of doing the thing that they do – as in, "I own a restaurant," or "I have landscape company." Instead, he says, "consider yourself in the marketing business of the thing you do." Michael Gerber would argue the same point and say, "we need to stop being the technicians doing the technical work of our business and instead work on the business." The transformation in your business will happen when you go from being a technician of the thing you do, to a marketer of the thing you do.

Not Just Marketing, but Marketing Systems

Once you have created the order fulfillment systems and the technical work of the business is on auto-pilot, your job is to become the master marketer - but not just marketing, marketing systems! You can approach marketing with the same predictable results to everything else your business delivers because of your systems.

Most businesses fail at marketing because they lack a systems approach. They engage in random acts of marketing and throw a bunch of stuff at the wall in hopes that something sticks.

Your marketing will be systemized to take a prospect along a path that is leading to a specific location – a closed sale. The lines get a little fuzzy as to what's marketing and what's sales, but the big idea is that most of both can be systemized. The easiest way to think of these two is that **lead generation is marketing systems and lead conversion is sales systems.**

> **Lead generation is marketing systems and lead conversion is sales systems.**

For the rest of this discussion let's focus our attention on marketing and lead generation systems and use the analogy of an equation. The formula to solve equations is the ideal example of systems. Another word for an equation is a problem – and if you use the same formula in the same way each time, using a step-by-step approach, you'll solve the problem. And there you have it, a system solution to a problem.

The Sales and Marketing Equation

Therefore, the marketing systems that will create these kinds of predictable results cannot be random, but must follow a path, an equation to be exact. The marketing equation is, Interrupt + Engage + Educate + Offer = Close. I first learned this as a sales equation in the Dale Carnegie Sales Course and they called it the The Five Great Rules of Selling: Attention, Interest, Conviction, Desire, Close (as found in the book by the same name by Percy Whiting, one of the first classic sales books). This further makes my point that the steps leading to a new customer are both selling and marketing, and they often overlap. Remember, that every step has to be used to solve the equation, every step has a purpose and is designed to follow a path to solve a problem – continual sales.

The sales/marketing equation is not new; it was first used in the early days of advertising when the purpose of a product was thoroughly thought through with a strategy and sales message. That was back when print advertising actually made sense and was often called, "salesmanship in print." Almost all print advertising today is hopelessly ineffective because it lacks these proven elements of the equation.

Let's take a few minutes to unpack each of the steps in the equation and discuss their purpose and why they're still the gold standard of effective selling and marketing.

Interrupt

Because of the vast amount of marketing clutter we have to break through, the first step is the hardest. But also, the interrupt has to get the prospects attention away from everything they're doing and thinking about, and for most busy executives, that's a lot. Today the bombardment of social media is yet another thing vying for our prospects precious time and attention. This explains why business owners who send out one postcard or one letter and get zero response say, "Oh I tried that and it doesn't work."

In marketing, the interrupt is a photo or image (usually of children, animals, or women in bikinis), or it could be the headline of an ad. In sales, it's the first words out of a salesperson's mouth. In both, it must be compelling and hold promise and hope to make the prospect's life better. The interrupt could also be more outrageous in nature, like a gift or lumpy mail or...let your imagination go crazy.

Recently I read the story of a business owner who built his entire sales presentation for his SEO marketing company around the celebrity of Justin Bieber and asked the question, "How can Justin Bieber help you grow your business?" To cut through the clutter and get his prospects attention, he sent his sales message in a package with a life size cutout of the Biebs himself. Now that's a great interrupt. To increase response he gave a discount if you sent back a picture with the cutout. Of the ten high profile prospects he targeted, six responded in 48 hours and four of them with a photo. To the four that didn't respond, he mailed another letter, this time with Justin Bieber's newly released album. One more responded, bringing his response rate to 70%. Again, the purpose of the interrupt is to break through.

Engage

The impact of the interrupt lasts seconds, and if you don't connect it to an engaging reason to learn more, you've lost your prospect. You have a picture of a scantily clad woman in your ad, so what, if it has nothing to do with your sales message to captivate me.

The interrupt gets attention, the engage step must speak plainly and quickly to the prospects pain or desires. Many marketers call it, "fear and greed," and argue all sales fall into those two categories. Another common sales maxim that gets to the heart of the engage step is, "*you can't sell John Smith what John Smith buys, until you can see the world through John Smith's eyes.*" What is John Smith,

> *"You can't sell John Smith what John Smith buys, until you can see the world through John Smith's eyes."*

your prospect, thinking about and what does he want or fear? This is also called Hot Button selling. To engage a prospect you have to speak to what's important to him or her, what's on their mind, what keeps them up a night.

These are their hot buttons, but you won't know what they are if you don't ask. The biggest mistake salespeople make is yakking on to the prospect all about their product and company, instead of simply asking, "What's the most important aspect of our service to you?" When you know the answer then you can effectively engage.

Educate

If you've really invested in the innovation of your business, if you've thought through again and again how to make your business better, if you have the most amazing inside reality of anyone in your industry, if you strive to hire the best people and train them to your systems... If, If, If...then, you must tell your prospects about it. If your business systems deliver a superior product and customer experience but you don't educate your prospects about it, they think your business is no better or no worse than any other company. The prospect's outside perception is that you're just as mediocre as the next guy, unless you tell him outright about your amazing inside reality.

Again, this is a marketing task and a sales task and can be identical messages – one delivered by media (print, web, video, etc.) and one delivered live and in person. Both can be systemized and automated but the marketing message is the easier one to control and hold accountable.

It's amazing how many salespeople shoot from the hip and don't work from a scripted sales presentation. That's what a sales presentation is – educating the prospect about why and exactly how your service is better. Don't expect your salespeople to do the heavy lifting of systemizing their sales presentation so that they deliver the same compelling message about your stellar services every single time. You have to create that system. Systemize as many pieces and parts of the sales presentation as possible. You should even be creating the sales scripts of exactly what the salesperson says and how they say it. See, I told you the marketing message is easier to control - which leads us into the Offer step of the equation.

Offer

Let me reiterate that marketing is salesmanship in print. It is conveying the same message in a compelling way to educate your prospect about your superior service. This, coupled with the prospect's desire to make the best buying decision is the formula for a great offer.

If your idea of an offer is a $5 off coupon or a 10% discount if you buy today, then you're missing your best opportunity for a superior position in your marketplace.

To educate the prospect, create an offer that not only makes you the authority, but provides a baby step to learn more about your company without the pressure of a salesperson coming to see you. Your offer can be a "buyer's guide" or a "special report" or even an article reprint or a book that makes the case for exactly what you sell.

"Makes the case," is the perfect way to think about your offer. Your business and what it sells is "on trial," you are the attorney and your prospects are the judge and jury who must decide in favor of your case. They must part with their money and buy.

Your marketing offer is an "information" offer to learn more and be educated; and most people like to be educated buyers. Offer your information guide in both online and offline formats and in all kinds of media.

Close

Whether it's in person or in your marketing message, someone must ask for the order. Let me say that again, ASK for the order! "Nothing happens until someone sells something," and all the previous steps in the equation are for naught if the sale doesn't close. The close must be the expectation from the beginning, so all the language and assumptions are leading to the reality of happily using our service. Therefore, when the "ask" comes, it's not awkward and unexpected, it's the natural next step in the process.

To create systems around this step, your process must make it simple to say, "Yes" and remove as many barriers as possible.

If you have an unconditional guarantee that removes all or most of the risk, that's making the sale simple. If you have payment options and easy terms, that's making it simple. If you have a vendor comparison guide that shows your company as the absolute best option, that's making it simple. All of these are innovations in the sales system and they can be created to make them automatic. Even the phrasing of the "ask" is a system and must be tweaked and tested until you get just the right response – "yes!"

Because this is not a book about marketing I must stop here – even though I'm tempted to write a chapter twice this size about marketing systems. You cannot delegate the marketing of your company. You need to become The marketing expert and apply this whole systems bent to your sales and marketing. If you'll go to www.MillerMarketingandConsulting.com you can download a Free report about The Ten Essentials for Creating Killer Marketing

Systems for Automatic Sales. After I share how each component can by systemized, I'll pull back the curtain and reveal our step-by-step "Gift Plant" marketing system that's gives us a "sufficient quantity and quality of leads on a continual and steady basis."

* For the full sales and marketing story and the definitive guide to creating lead generation and lead conversion systems, look for the soon to be released, ***"Victory Goes to the Business with Superior Marketing Systems."***

CHAPTER 7

Knowing Your Numbers

Systemizing the Management and Measuring Process

"Whatever you measure, improves."

- Peter Drucker

When your business is small and you're the only employee, the need to measure your performance is not a big deal. You have a pretty good idea of how productive you're...No! Wait! **Stop!**

Ok, that's how I began this chapter, but after reading it over, it just didn't ring true. The idea that if you are the only employee there's not a need for managing yourself and measuring your results is just not true.

If you're not keeping good records of your work performance, output and time logs, there's a really good chance you're deceiving yourself. Deceiving yourself to make yourself look and feel better of course!

What's the big deal you say? The big deal is, you may think you're making money and huge profits, and you may believe you're highly productive but even in a one person operation, without accurate, honest measuring you could be fooling yourself. So here's the new start to this chapter:

Management and measuring systems are the tools that will give you the greatest gains in time and productivity (read profit), no matter what size your business, *especially* if you're a one-person operation. You can't just guess, have a hunch, or trust your gut; you need solid data. Reports and forms that systematically collect "real life data" of what's going on in the day to day, 9 to 5, of your business not only keeps you honest, it also spurs you (and your team) on to beat your best.

If you're trying to run your business without the systems to measure your daily efforts, it's kinda like our new age ideal of teaching our kids to play baseball without keeping score. Nobody gets their feelings hurt or has to feel inferior because their performance doesn't measure up. In the same way, we can be blissfully ignorant in our belief that our business is more successful than it really is and that we're making more money than we really are.

> **"If you can't measure it, you can't manage it."**

If the average small business owner really calculated how many hours they worked each week against their take home pay, they might be shocked to realize their lowest paid employee is probably making more per hour than them. That's why I love that quote by Drucker, "If you can't measure it, you can't manage it." You have to figure out a simple system for measuring everything that really matters to the bottom line. Nothing matters more to the bottom line than sales.

Sales measuring and management

Once, I hired a salesperson that came with a great reputation for his sales ability. We mistakenly relied too heavily on his sales superstar status and didn't require weekly activity reports. Oops, bad mistake.

After he had been selling for almost 5 months with us – uh, correction, after he'd been not selling much for 5 months, we created a new weekly sales activity report.

The sales report required that he add at least 10 new prospects into our marketing funnel, make a minimum of 3 appointments, write at least 2 proposals and close a certain dollar amount of new sales.

Wow, what an immediate change, not only in activity, but more importantly, results – as in closed sales!

We wanted to be completely invested in his success, because when he scored, we scored; but without the ability to measure what he was doing we couldn't really manage his efforts and help him do better. That's the beauty of measuring so that you can manage, because as Drucker says, "Whatever you measure, improves."

When you start a conversation about reports, tracking data, financial statements, etc., chances are you just lost a bunch of the shoot-from-the-hip entrepreneurial types - they can't be bothered with such stuff. They'd rather go sell something or create something than sit and analyze reports and data. Yeah, I get that! Which is precisely why your management and measuring has to be systemized. Instead of pages of data and piles of reports, think dashboards.

Business Dashboards

Of course if you drive a car you know what a dashboard is, but think what a dashboard does to give information to the driver of the vehicle. It's a snapshot look at the most important systems that affect the car's performance: fuel level, engine temperature, speedometer, etc. The driver doesn't have to stop and look under the hood and run engine diagnostics to know how the car is performing, it's all present, right there on the dashboard.

> **Key Performance Indicators (KPIs) enable instantaneous and informed decisions to be made at a glance."**

Here's the same idea applied to business from Peter McFadden, CEO of ExcelDashboardWidgets:

*"An easy to read, often single page, real-time user interface, showing a graphical presentation of the current status (snapshot) and historical trends of an organization's **key performance indicators** (KPIs) to enable instantaneous and informed decisions to be made at a glance."*

The key distinctions here are "single page, real-time, easy to read, snapshot" and "informed decisions." Your business dashboard will give you the quick information you need to manage your business better.

Instead of piles of reports that sit unread, the purpose of the dashboard is "at a glance" information for quick decisions.

When you're driving your car and see the fuel gauge on the dashboard is pointing to "E," you make the "informed decision" to stop driving and get fuel.

You are the *driver* of your business and as such, you're responsible for its performance and without a dashboard of the key performance indicators (KPI's) you may drive it into a ditch.

There's a popular show on Food Network called *Restaurant Stake Out* where a restaurant consultant named Willie Degel (who also owns his own restaurants) comes in to help struggling restaurant owners. His team sets up hidden cameras to get an idea of what's "really" going on when the owner is away.

On one episode Degel is asking question after question about a restaurant owner's operation, all of which the poor, bewildered restaurant guy has no answer for. Degel peppers him with, "What's your daily customer count? What's your average sale per customer? What are the sales for each day? What's the most popular item on the menu? What's the most profitable item on the menu?" You can see the restaurant owner getting perturbed and incredulous that anyone could really know the answer to all that stuff.

Then to drive his point home Degel whips out his cell phone and immediately calls one of his own restaurants. The first system he had in place was an amazing greeting to the caller, "Good afternoon, this is Julie, thank you for calling *"Uncle Jack's Steakhouse,"* how can I help you?"

But more to the point, he simply says, "Hi Julie, it's me."

Degel then gets treated to an amazing verbal dashboard of his restaurant for that specific day and time. Without his even asking, Julie reports, "Hi Willie, there are currently about xx people in the dining room, the sales for the day are $xx.xx, the customer count for the day is xx, and we have xx reservations for tonight."

Those kinds of management systems don't have to be cumbersome and time consuming. That whole conversation took less than 30 seconds and Degel had a good pulse of his restaurant's health that day. No, you don't need hours to pour over reports, but you do need intention, just like any other system you'd create. Again, make sure you're not collecting data that doesn't move the needle in a significant way. Think, Key Performance Indicators.

To tie a ribbon on these last three chapters, the things that really need to be managed and measured will most likely relate to order fulfillment (delivering the goods) and sales and marketing (lead generation and lead conversion). If you can create the systems that measure these, you'll really enjoy watching them improve.

CHAPTER 8

Your Life and Your Business Imagined

The Value of Vision PART I

Create the vision of the *life* you want, then create a business that makes that life reality

"Where there is no vision the people perish."

- **Proverbs 29:18**

When Dr. Ken McCaffrey started his practice he knew exactly the kind of patient experience he wanted to create. He envisioned a warm and friendly, healing environment where patients felt more like guests at a fine hotel. So when he began to create his business systems, he didn't copy doctors' offices down the street; instead he copied the guest experience at the top luxury hotels.

Instead of patients being handed a clipboard through a glass window, his staff comes out into the lobby, sits down beside the patient (or should they be called a guest), and asks them questions in a kind personal manner. Dr. McCaffrey has scripted as much of the new patient experience as possible. His staff is trained to focus on the *patient and their health*, not "who is your insurance company?" The patients of his practice are asked to be seated in the lobby (with finely appointed décor, subdued lighting, and live plants), not *wait in the waiting room*. Appointment times are honored and patients are greeted (on time) by a smiling staff person who comes into the lobby to meet them personally - unlike most Doctor's offices where you must wait in the sterile waiting room for an hour past your appointment time, only to have your last name shouted from the door like your order is ready at a busy BBQ joint – and this by a nurse who's harried and hurried.

Dr. McCaffrey's advertising and marketing has a specific phone number, so that his staff knows when a potential new client is calling - they are instructed and trained (with scripts) to focus on that first impression. The potential new patient is their top priority along with their questions and concerns. In addition, these phone calls are recorded for training purposes and Dr. McCaffrey, or his lead administrator, listen to these phone calls to ensure that the systems are being followed properly.

Another one of his signature systems is a personal handwritten note to a patient, wishing them good health and a quick recovery - from him. A personal note may not seem like much of a system - but when integrated into the whole patient experience, the results are amazing.

He tells the story of a patient who with tears in her eyes said, "I have never received a handwritten note from a doctor. Thank You for caring about my health."

How did Dr. McCaffrey create these systems? He envisioned

exactly how he wanted his patients to feel, what he wanted them to see, and what he wanted them to hear. He envisioned the kind of healing, patient experience that he would want for himself. **But before that,** he created the vision he wanted for his life and his family (and it didn't include 70 hour work weeks, 40 to 50 patients a day, with less than 10 minutes for each).

Then, and only then, could he go to work to create the systems for the business he imagined – so that his business could fulfill the vision he had for his life.

Stop and read that last sentence again. You cannot create the systems to make the kind of life and business that you want, until you have a very clear vision. A detailed picture of how your life will look and how the business will work when it is fully functioning and doing what it does, with excellence.

Another great analogy for this idea of *"vision first, then completed product"* are the architectural blueprints required to build a fine custom home.

Over 20 years ago my wife and I built our dream home. In the year leading up to the construction, we paid an architect to sit with us as we described every detail of how we wanted our home to look, inside and outside. We gave him as much detail as possible of how we like to live, our plans for growing a family, how we like to use our house to entertain, and all our likes and dislikes. Then he went to work.

He took all the details of our vision of the home we wanted and created the architectural blueprints – with immense and vast detail (make note of that: *immense and vast detail*). The first page of the blueprints was the elevation – the front driveway view of how the home would look when it was completed. That completed view (make note of that too: *completed view*), made our hearts race with excitement as we could see ourselves living there and enjoying our home.

Behind the completed view were pages and pages of details for the different trades that were going to build the home. Plumbing and electrical and carpentry trades all had their own sections in the big pile of blueprint pages. Their work was integrated with each other because they were all working off the same set of blueprints – they were all working together, doing very different work with the same goal and a common vision – our home, exactly as we had described it, and as the architect drafted it.

Does that get you excited when you think of your business? It should! This is exactly how you must think of your business! You must act as the architect - the visionary of what your business will look like, with **immense and vast detail** - when it is **completed.** And there's no possible way you can enlist the help of all "the trades," (your team of employees), if they don't have their own set of blueprints to work from.

"Where there is no vision, the people perish." This verse from King Solomon is also translated, "where there is no vision, the people cast off restraint." Without a clear and definitive vision from the leader, the people, (your people) resort to doing whatever seems right to them. Strong leadership is required in any enterprise, and that begins with a vision.

Compare the trades of plumbing, electrical, and carpentry to the varying departments in your business. Every business has some departments that are the same: a sales department, a customer service department, and a finance and accounting department, for example. But you'll also have departments that are unique for your industry and your business. Every person in each of these departments must have their own strategic vision, so they know how their daily tasks fit together, to achieve the overall company vision.

> Until you complete the creative, vision work of exactly how you want to live your life - you can't do the process work of creating the systems to make it happen.

You as the business owner must take ownership of this – you must be the one who is creating the blueprints for your business and the blueprints for each individual department. That's going to work on the business, to innovate and create the exact customer experience that differentiates you from all other options and competitors. That's what Dr. McCaffrey did with his practice and that's what you must learn to master as well.

Listen, until you complete the creative, vision work of exactly how you want to live your life, and how your business will serve that life – meaning how your business will look, feel and flow, you can't do the process work of creating the systems to make it happen.

My Pitfalls of No Vision

Working without a strategic vision is all too familiar to me, especially when I think back on the early days of acquiring our business property for our greenhouse operation. The piece of land I found was the dream property I had been searching for and praying for - only better than I could have imagined. The dream home I described above had a wonderful and unexpected surprise that we found when we cleared the lot for its construction. Behind all the trees and underbrush we discovered a three-and-a-half acre grass field, adjacent to our backyard. It was impossible to see from the front of our lot because the underbrush was so thick, but it was a blank-slate piece of property with only one pine tree and grass that was mowed by the owner who had a house on the front one acre.

When I saw it I was excited, but for all the wrong reasons, "What a great field this will be to play Frisbee with the dog." Yes, that's right, that was my big grand vision for this property. No vision for a business property or a greenhouse operation, just a simple visualization of a man and his dog playing Frisbee.

Long story short, the owner was eager to sell the back two acres of this property (which was zoned agricultural) and even gave me an access, off of a side street. Ultimately, this enabled our business to have its own address and entry drive. I can walk to work from my backyard, but our staff drive in. I told you, it was my dream business property, only exceedingly and abundantly more than I could ask or imagine!

With two acres to develop and only needing one small shade house structure, I was still seriously lacking a vision for the property. Without this vision, not just for the property and its future use, but more importantly for the day-to-day operation, it soon became a jumbled mess of unbelievable proportions. It embarrasses me to admit how bad my greenhouse property really was, but this was years before my systems revolution.

Our slogan is "Plants and Planters – Guaranteed Gorgeous." Our service is guaranteed plant care - so that means on any week we have a truck load of gorgeous new plants going out as replacements for those that are not – and the not-so-gorgeous plants coming back to the greenhouse, in a wide range of variety and health.

Without going into more painful detail about how out of control our greenhouse operation really was, just imagine an automobile junkyard, and replace the smashed up cars and car parts with plants! It was an experience I never want to repeat, but it was a lesson I'll never forget about how out of control and haphazard something can get, without the systems and vision to guide the operation.

The story has another great lesson, and this is the one I love to tell – the story of an amazing greenhouse operation that processes hundreds of plants, each week, in a stunningly clean and organized environment. Our greenhouse property is "Tournament Ready" (a term used by golf course superintendents) 90% of the time, so that we can use it as a marketing tool and invite prospects to come take a tour. If we can get a potential new customer to come see our operation – the gorgeous plants and planters, the grounds, the order and processes – we close the deal. That's the power of a vision realized and the systems development process that makes it happen.

My wife, Crystal and I saw our shared vision for our new home every day as we went off to work. We wanted a good reminder of what we were working towards, so we took the first page of the blueprints, the one with the picture of our dream home when it was complete, and we posted it on the laundry room door. This was our exit to the garage as we went off to work and we saw it every day. Where there is no vision the people perish and without a vision there's no power to do the hard work to make it come to reality.

The next step is to, "Write the vision; make it plain on tablets, so he may run who reads it."

CHAPTER 9

Your Life and Your Business Vision Becoming Reality

The Value of Vision Part II

From Big Vision to Daily Tasks and Systems

"Write the vision; make it plain on tablets, so he may run who reads it."

- Habakkuk 2:2

As the title of this chapter suggests, our purpose is to move from the big vision of who, what, and why the business is, to the daily tasks of how to make that happen. This is a logical progression from big picture to smaller, becoming more specific and detailed with each step. Imagine this process as an inverted pyramid with the large side at the top and the point at the bottom. The "steps" start at the top and step down the pyramid.

The top of the pyramid represents the large over-arching vision of your business – it is your "strategic vision statement." It is a general statement but it is at the same time, all encompassing. The

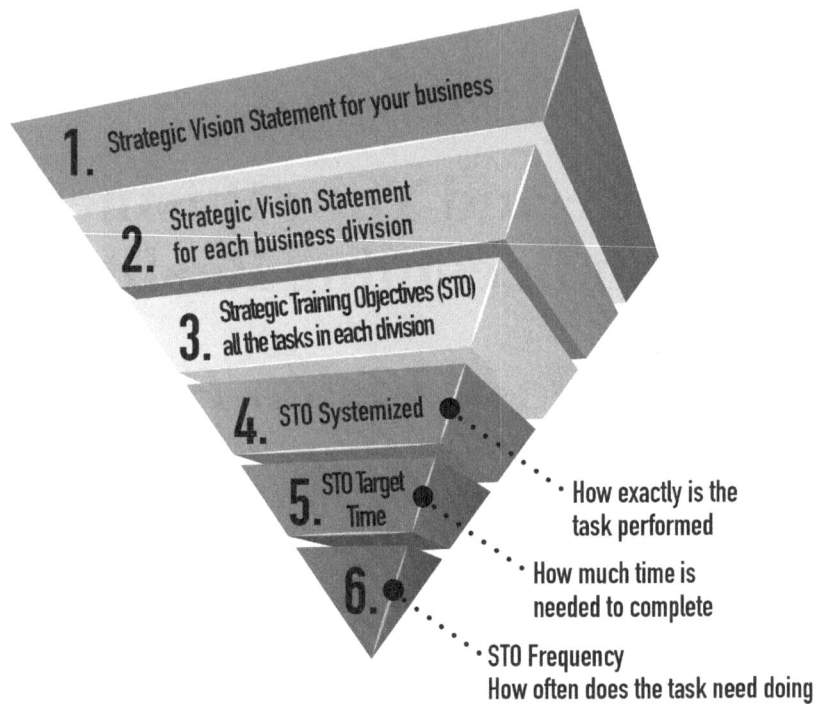

pyramid narrows as the description of what the business does and how it operates comes to the point. At the bottom of the pyramid are the specific descriptions of the systems: how to do them (system documentation), how often (frequency), and how long each should take (target time).

This is why it's essential to start with the strategic vision – because you can't describe, in precise detail, what to do at the systems operational level if you don't know exactly what the vision is you are trying to fulfill.

It would be like my wife and I building our dream home and asking the plumber, electrician, and carpenter to show up and get straight to work without giving them a set of blueprints. The legitimate and obvious question from each would be, "Go to work on what?"

The strategic vision statement is a plain language, decision guiding map that keeps everyone on task and heading in the same direction. It keeps all work focused on the accomplishment of a common goal. The vision must be written down and made plain so that everyone who reads it, fully understands how their work on any given day contributes to the company's ability to serve people.

"Write the vision; make it plain on tablets, so he may run who reads it."

- Habakkuk 2:2

If you want your business to ***run,*** to boldly make swift progress, if you want your team to ***run*** and avoid the pitfalls of burnout because they feel their work is drudgery, then you need to invest wholeheartedly in your company's strategic vision. Remember the goal of this is to make it simple, write it down, and teach each staff person how their work contributes to the fulfillment of the overall strategic vision of the business.

Wait, don't skip this step! If you're anything like me, you may be tempted to bag some of this "thinking work" and get to the daily task list. I have a very low threshold for things concerning the Mission Statement and Vision Statement, and would much rather just dive in, get to work and figure all that other stuff out later (you've just learned in the last chapter from my greenhouse fiasco the results of that approach).

This reminds me of a quote from the infamous business guru, George Carlin:

"Some people see things that are and ask, why? Some people dream of things that never were and ask, Why not? Some people have to go to work and don't have time for all that."

Listen closely business friend, resist the urge to merely go back to work and skip this whole vision step – you've got to make time "for all that." Experience has taught me the value of investing in this vital step in the process before the work – and so I guarantee you this will be of immense value to you. Another promise I'll make is to keep it practical and task oriented, knowing you have work to do and customers to serve.

From Vision to Systemized Daily Tasks

Step 1. Strategic Vision Statement – for your business

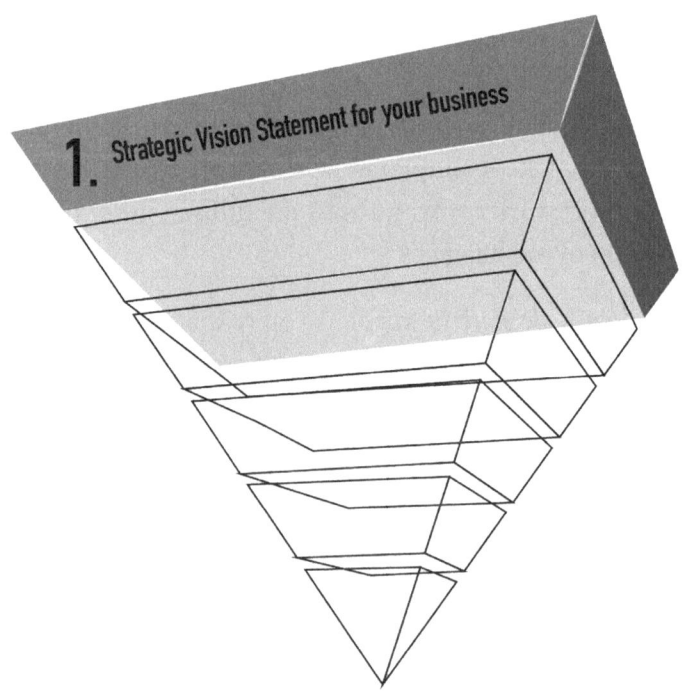

For my business, greenhouse operations is obviously just part of the story, joining with the other nine divisions of the company. They all integrate and merge for the ultimate purpose of completing the company's overall strategic vision.

This is your starting line. Your company's strategic vision should answer the questions of who exactly do you serve and how do you serve them. This statement should cause you to dig deep and sweat a little. If it's too easy to write this the first time, you probably don't have it. When you do have it you should have an "aha, eureka, I've found it" moment and you should have some emotion and passion invested in it. After all, this is your work and how you best serve other people.

Here is my Vision Statement and another I like to get your creative juices flowing:

Strategic Vision: Interior Plant Scapes is the premier provider in Southwest Florida for creating ambience and beautiful spaces for people, using gorgeous live plants in decorative containers and guaranteeing their continuous beauty with professional plant care – in a manner that honors God.

This one is from Moorings Park, an upscale retirement community in Naples, Florida:

Moorings Park is the premier provider in Southwest Florida of services, facilities and health support, to enable successful aging.

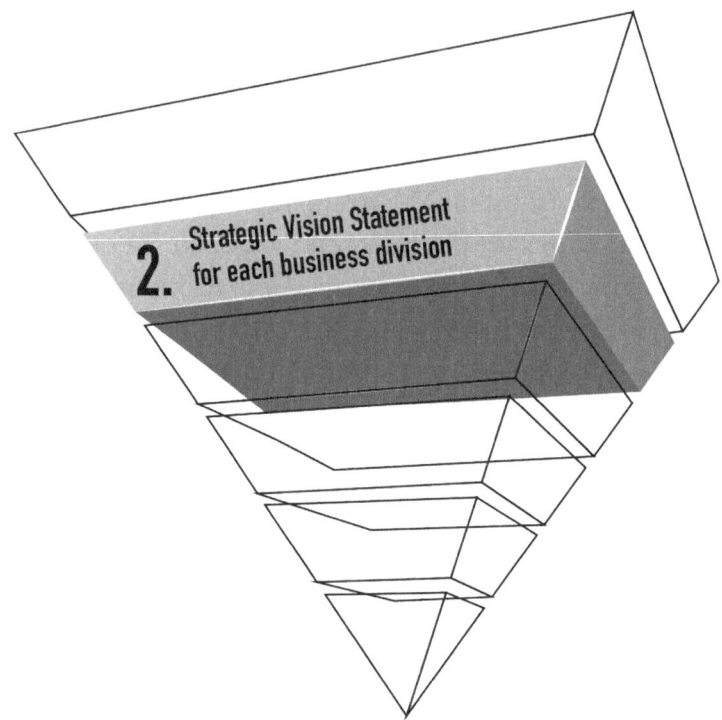

As I've previously mentioned, the divisions for each company will vary based on your industry and business type. The divisions of your company will grow and expand as your business does. We never had a separate *order fulfillment department* that preps all plants for new installations, until we were doing 3 to 4 installs a week, which made it necessary.

The strategic vision by division is important because every employee must comprehend it and get excited by how their daily tasks, whether raking the driveway or making deposits, contributes to the company's goals.

Here are the 10 divisions of *Interior Plant Scapes*:

Strategic Vision by Division:

1. Staff Development – Our People
2. Finance and Accounting – Our Profit
3. Marketing – Our Presentation
4. Sales – Our Proposition
5. Greenhouse – Our Product and Property
6. Order Fulfillment - Our Preparation for Success
7. Delivery and Installation – Our Primary Impression
8. Plant Care – Our Product and Service
9. Quality Assurance – Our Performance Measured
10. Office Administration – Our Promises Kept

The Greenhouse Division

Our greenhouse gardener, Gary, is the perfect example of the amazing results you can achieve when you successfully combine hard work with effective systems.

Gary was the farthest thing from lazy you've ever seen, and because he was Cuban, his drink of choice, not just in the morning, but all day, was Cuban coffee. This was like rocket fuel for Gary and gave him the extra gas to jump in and tackle his work with gusto. Gary's problem though was lack of focus and the inability to prioritize his work based on the company goals and needs of our client's plants. He'd get jacked up on caffeine and go off in every direction, except the strategic vision of the greenhouse division.

My goal for Gary (and with every staff member) was to harness his gusto and energy and channel it in a way that served the overall company through his division – the greenhouse. That begins with the strategic vision for the greenhouse. The greenhouse strategic vision was something I had to revisit with Gary often:

Greenhouse – Our Product and Property

Healthy Plants are Foundational to everything we do, therefore, our greenhouse operation is an amazing integration of systems that consistently deliver the *highest quality plants* in a *stunningly clean environment*.

With a strategic vision statement like that, you can quickly surmise that we were going to do our work of providing gorgeous plants with systems. No haphazard, shoot-from-the-hip approach to the greenhouse work, but rather a tight schedule of what exactly has to be done and when.

This was not flawless in keeping Gary focused on what really mattered to the day-to-day operations of the greenhouse. His bent was to be building something or doing low level busy work that anyone could do. My bent was the Strategic vision of the greenhouse: *High quality plants in a stunningly clean environment.* Many times Gary should have been checking irrigation to ensure proper watering or spraying for pests and disease, but he would rather reorganize the tool barn. Strategic vision focuses and prioritizes the work into the Strategic Training Objectives, the next step down the pyramid.

To see the Strategic Vision Statements for each Interior Plant Scapes division – go to www.MillerMarketingandConsulting.com

Step 3. Strategic Training Objectives – all the tasks in each division

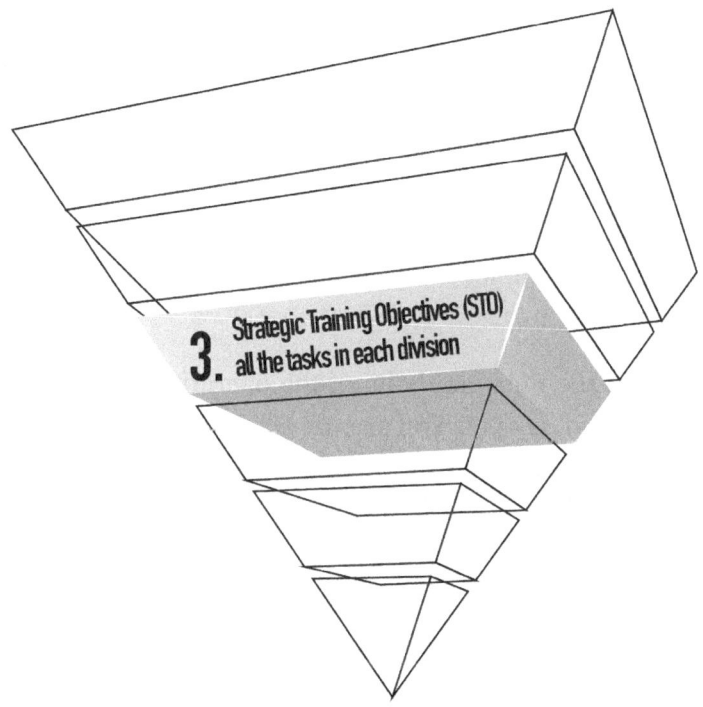

With two acres of "possible" projects and thousands of plants to care for, it's easy to see why it's difficult for Gary to stay on track. Unless...unless you have a system that lists all of the tasks that need to be done - we call those Strategic Training Objectives (STO's).

STO's are the answer to what *exactly* has to be done, to accomplish the strategic vision in that division. For the greenhouse division we have 37 different STO's. Not all have to be done every day and some only happen once or twice a year (more about frequency in a later step down the pyramid). **Imagine that the**

STO's create *a business within the business* for every division. So, for the greenhouse "business," what are the 37 different tasks that are responsible for achieving the Greenhouse Strategic Vision - "the highest quality plants in a stunningly clean environment?"

Of course each division is working for the goals of the whole company, but at the same time there are tasks and systems that are wholly unique to each division. Those systems must be documented so that each new employee can learn to perform the tasks impeccably and consistently.

STO's are the nuts and bolts of the operation that get the job done, day in and day out. You are not writing the system yet, **and you aren't describing "the how" to do it – you are describing "the what" needs to be done.**

Here is a partial list of some of the Greenhouse STO's:

1. Greenhouse Walk-Through
2. Drip Irrigation Check, Emitters, and Filters
3. Sub-Irrigation Up-potting
4. Weed Control Techniques
5. Prune Ficus Tree Rentals
6. Planting (up-potting) New Plants
7. Unpack Bromeliads and Stock
8. Service and Wash Delivery Trucks
9. Clean, Groom, and Organize Greenhouse 3

When describing the tasks for each division, be super specific and don't generalize. Instead of saying, *"clean the greenhouse grounds"* break it into smaller systems that can be described and documented like:

1. Clean and organize the entry drive
2. Weed control techniques
3. Office landscape maintenance
4. Dumpster area organization
5. Nursery pot storage area

Each one of these is part of the section titled, **clean the greenhouse grounds**, but there are standards and systems for each. The standards come from my vision of how the greenhouse grounds should look (since we are in the business of creating curb appeal and sense of arrival, it would be hypocritical if our grounds didn't create some sense of Wow).

> **You can't build the dream house if the blueprints are only stored in your head.**

Yes, I have a vision for how the greenhouse grounds should look, but if it's only in my head and not intimately described to others there's no way anyone can help me achieve it. You can't build the dream house if the blueprints are only stored in your head.

Step 4. Strategic Training Objective (STO) Systemized – how exactly the task is performed

This is what you've been waiting for! Taking your big vision and creating the daily tasks to see it come into reality – in the way *you* have envisioned it! That's the key – Your Vision of how your business works, not your staff's idea or anyone else's.

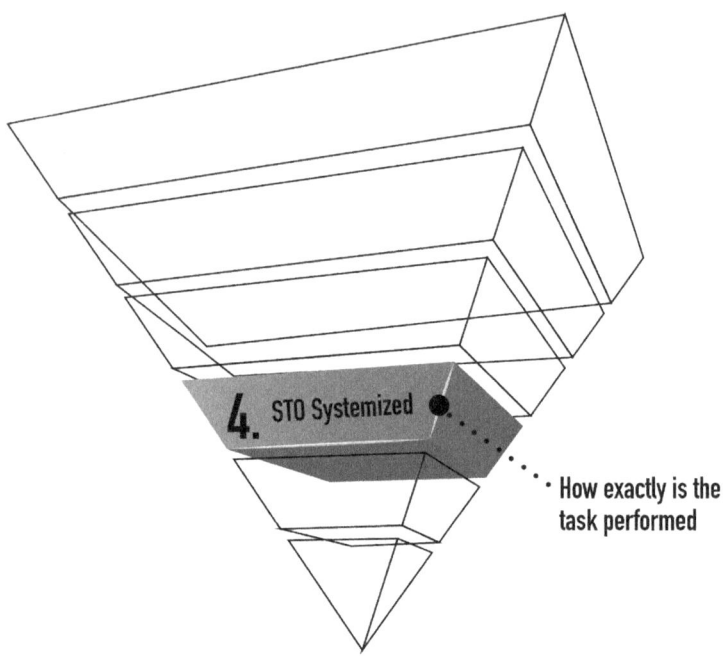

Again, Gary was the kind of worker any employer would want, eager to jump in and work hard at any task, but without proper instruction and a specific procedure, he would quickly go off the rails. Not only would he work on the wrong task at the wrong time (failure to prioritize) but he would complete the task the wrong way (failure to systemize).

The systemization magic happens when you begin to drill down into every task in every division and design and innovate every task so that not only is the work predictable and duplicatable, it's efficient and profitable. That's leveraging "ordinary people with extraordinary systems." In the next chapter I'll go into the exact detail of how to "design and innovate" every task.

Step 5. Strategic Training Objective – Target Time

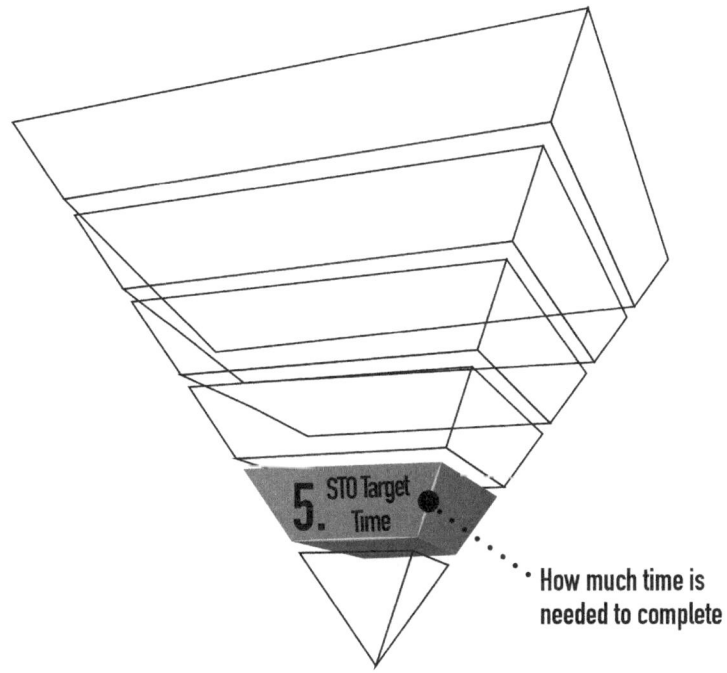

Time is _____! Everyone knows the answer - money. This is where your investment in systems creation will reap great rewards. Because labor is always one of the top one or two items on a P&L, work must be completed within a predetermined time budget – we call that a target time. Without target times your simplest systems will fall victim to Parkinson's Law – "work expands to fill the time allotted for its completion." If you give someone an hour to complete a task that should only require 10 minutes, somehow that task magically grows.

That's the main reason why target times are essential for systems building - target time gives vital information to the person doing the task. By documenting that this task should take 20 minutes, the one doing the task now knows if they're doing it correctly. If the target time is one hour for a task and I finish it in five minutes, quite frankly I've missed something. Likewise, if I can't complete a task within the allotted target time, either the target time is wrong or I don't understand and haven't been properly trained on the system.

A recurring task at the greenhouse is up-potting plants. We buy smaller pot size plants and then "up-pot" them using our Sub-Irrigation system. Some weeks there are hundreds of incoming plants to up-pot.

Invariably when we train a new person on our Up-potting System they take about 3 to 5 minutes to plant one plant; this is even after they have seen our system and technique. Then we drill down more and show them all the extra fussing and primping that's completely unnecessary when up-potting plants and we shave off precious minutes from the task.

From start to finish, using our system, we teach people to up-pot a plant in 45 seconds or less. A minute or two saved may not seem like much, but multiply that by hundreds of plants and it's huge.

Step 6. Strategic Training Objective – Frequency

The frequency of the task is another piece of information that really aids and informs the person doing the work.

Depending on the task, the system can be created to provide the essential consistency and predictability to your business functions. Business is nothing if it isn't predictable and consistent. Some tasks

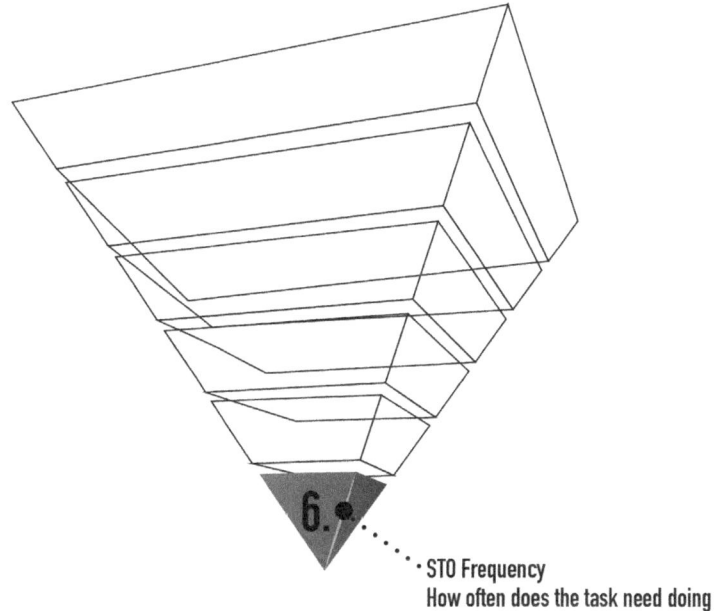

STO Frequency
How often does the task need doing

need to be done once a day (or more), others once a week, and others merely once a year. Whatever the frequency of the task is, the fact that it is systemized to happen with that frequency is a integral part of making that system work.

This is exactly how the airline industry is able to deliver thousands and thousands of passengers, safely and routinely, to their destinations every day. Every plane has thorough standards of maintenance and safety checks that happen on a specific schedule. The frequency standard of these checklists is what keeps the planes in the air and give us amazing confidence to fly.

Now, let's go to work and really begin to design and innovate the systems to create the business (and the life) you have imagined.

CHAPTER 10

11 Rules and Reminders for Designing and Innovating Your Systems

"Your systems are perfectly designed for the results you're getting."

- Pat Morley

In 1972, Fisher Price introduced a clothing line that created a brand new way to think about children and clothes. It was a breakthrough pairing system, using mix-and-match separates, that was so easy to use that young children could select their own clothes and dress themselves. The kid-friendly Garanimals clothing line not only freed up mom and dad from getting the kids ready in the morning, more importantly perhaps, it developed the child's early feelings of self-confidence through small decisions and accomplishments. Garanimals clothes used pictures of animals to teach a child what shirt or blouse went with what skirt or pants. Grab a monkey shirt along with a monkey skirt and you have a fool-proof and fun way to get yourself dressed. Wow, can you say, "Innovation?"

Even Dr. Joyce Brothers loved the system, "Garanimals...helps the preschooler to handle his/her wardrobe. That sense of 'I Can' fosters the child's growing sense of independence."

If you really believe there's no opportunity in your business for systems and innovation (because of course, "my business is different"), if you struggle with the thought of creating new systems strategies and break-through ideas...stop and think about Garanimals. Who would have thought you could innovate and systemize children's clothing? This is the epitome of, "creating extraordinary systems that can be used by ordinary people." This is a goal to keep in mind: creating systems that are so good (as in simple) and state-of-the-art that your business consistently and predictably delivers superior results in the hands of your staff people. As an aside to Garanimals, why hasn't someone created the 50 year old guy version? We all know men (and women I guess) who desperately need a Lion on their shirt to match the Lion on their pants...and tie, socks and shoes as well.

Yes, there is opportunity in your business for systems breakthroughs. What is the equivalent of Garanimals for your order fulfillment systems? How can you create systems that are "so easy, even a caveman could do it?"

The purpose of this chapter is to give you very practical, nuts-and-bolts ideas so that you actually put systems to use in your business – I call them the...

11 Rules and Reminders for Creating and Innovating Your Systems

1. Document Everything

It really is not a system until it's documented. Just because you have a cool process of how a piece of your business works, doesn't mean anything, unless you have it documented. You heard me say early on in the book that you want to get the business out of your head and into procedural manuals. The purpose of procedural manuals is immense as we've discussed, but let me emphasize again that the only thing worse than having your business in your head (and not on paper), is having your business floating around in an employee's head. This is a common, yet tragic problem in small business; the employer is held captive by mediocre or incompetent employees. He or she is afraid to fire a problem employee because the employee knows more about certain aspects of the business than the owner does. This leads to all kinds of misbehavior and indulgences from entitled staff members.

> **It's not a system until it's documented.**

Of course, without documented systems, it's nearly impossible to effectively train new hires, and more important, to enforce your systems. Documenting all the systems and procedures in your business is a freeing experience that allows a business owner to show the "problem child" to the door, and fill the position with a more suitable and enthusiastic person.

But documenting systems doesn't just mean the written word – there are numerous ways to document your systems.

2. Use Pictures Liberally

One night instead of ordering pizza for delivery, I called in the order for take-out and picked it up myself. What an awesome systems lesson I had during the ten minute wait for my pizza to be finished. This was a small Papa John's delivery and take-out only shop, so you could stand at the front counter and watch the whole pizza-making operation. There were full-color 8 by 10 photos everywhere. The wall where the pizzas were made had the most pictures and little to no words. The pictures were the system! Just in case you missed that, I repeat, "The pictures were the system!" You could see, by comparing the pictures on the wall to the pie you were making, if you were doing it right.

Make sure you use lots of pictures to help document your systems. Use before and after pictures, use right and wrong pictures (the wrong picture could have a big red X across it), use step by step pictures that show the process in progress. Whatever areas you can think of that should have pictures, display them. Which leads into another important systems creation rule.

3. Think Step By Step

Many systems are a process and involve several steps. If there are a lot of steps in the system, make sure you document each step. The steps could be a series of pictures only or it could be pictures with captions and directions for each step. If you've ever bought unassembled furniture you've had a lesson in a step by step system with pictures and directions (and you've had a good lesson in patience). If you break the system down into the most logical "next" step and think "this, then this" – you'll have a wonderful transferable task that's easily teachable.

4. Assume Nothing

When creating your Step by Step system make for sure that you Assume Nothing. In the chapter on Micro Manage to the Max, you were challenged to be the inventor and creator of the customer experience for your business. Your systems have to include the most minute details of how you want the customer to feel, what you want them to see (and not see), what you want them to hear, etc. Hear me when I say, if you don't design and document precisely how you want your business to operate, then your staff will make it up on their own. Your business (and your customer's experience) will be sacrificed at the whim and preference of your employees. Disney is the epitome of this rule. Disney assumes nothing and has definitive standards for how "cast members" should look (no facial hair for men and uniforms for everyone), speak and relate to guests. Every detail in the parks is either on-stage or back-stage - and they are sticklers that a guest should never see a back-stage area.

> **Micro Manage to the Max.**

5. A Glossary of Terms

As you can tell from the above, Disney has their own lingo too, as every business should. Every industry has terms that are unique to their business and training a new hire should include memorizing the Glossary of Terms. Having distinct definitions for every tool, process, location, and position not only lets staff know you're serious about your business – it also eliminates a massive amount of mistakes and do-overs. Instead of asking someone to load "the brown thingamajig with the black handle" – have a published and agreed upon name for it to stop the confusion. We use saucers and liners inside of our decorative containers – two similar but different products. The cost differential is five times or more – a 14 inch clear vinyl saucer is $1.75, a comparable liner is $12.00. We make sure everyone knows the difference! Another example is the industry standard name for the staff who care for plants in client accounts – "Plant Care Technicians," or Techs for short. Years ago I changed that to Gardeners, to better describe the professionalism and persona of what we really do. In my mind, Technicians work on A/C units and cars, Gardeners care for beautiful, living, breathing plants that create gorgeous ambiance.

6. Systems Require Memorization (Your Business Should Too)

Clearly, if you're going to have a glossary of terms, then you expect your staff to memorize the names and definitions. Memorization work and expectations should be part of your training manual, with detailed lists of what by when (what should be memorized by what date). When I started working as a waiter, I could not get onto the floor (meaning I was relegated to bus-boy status) until I could answer key questions about the menu and ingredients of each entrée. In addition, I was expected to recite, from memory, the exact ingredients for table-side preparation of Caesar salad, Wilted Spinach salad, Veal Marsala and Bananas Foster. The training worked (and stuck – I can still make a mean Caesar from scratch)!

Memorization is part of training and should be expected of every position. If you're not requiring memorization as part and parcel of employment with your company, your expectations are too low. At my company, *Interior Plant Scapes*, we use only about 30 different varieties of tropical plants and that in itself is an innovation through years of trial, error, and success with the very best plants, for every application (Prior to the development of systems, *Interior Plant Scapes* used over 60 different plants and many of them losers.) A memorization system we require of every new hire is the 3-letter plant code for every one of the 30 plants we use. The plant code is an essential tool for every department and learning all of them is just one of several systems we not only expect everyone to learn – but to memorize.

7. Use Checklists Liberally

If you want to see a terrific lesson using systems to transform a failing business, watch *Hotel Impossible*, a reality TV show starring Anthony Melchiori. This guy is amazing in his ability to quickly cut through the bull and surmise the core problems of failing hotels. Hotel owners or GM's contact him and ask for his help, so when he comes in he doesn't have to tap dance like a paid consultant who's afraid of losing their consulting gig. Melchiorri is well-mannered and unbelievably patient with disillusioned hotel staff, but he sugar coats nothing! Most amazing and instructive to me is that many of the problems in these failing hotels are system failures. One of Melchior's favorite systems tools is checklists. Of course the hotel maids should be using a room's checklist while cleaning (many are not), but he uses checklists as a major management tool through-out the whole hotel. Not only hotels, my friend, but every business should have series of checklists - here are just a few:

- ➢ Opening and closing duties
- ➢ Property standards – inside and out
- ➢ New customer/account set up
- ➢ Loading for installations of any kind
- ➢ Party or event set-ups

Maybe, right now you're saying, "duh, of course you use checklists," but it's amazing how many business don't, and I'll betcha dollars to donuts there are areas of your business right now that need the sure discipline of a checklist system.

8. Systemization Not Organization

If you remember my kitchen closet story from chapter 2, you know the difference between organization and systemization. Organization is removing the clutter and bringing order to a chaotic work area or process. Systemization is innovating the "why and how" a work space or process should work for maximum efficiency. As I explained previously, my wife and I have a large walk-in kitchen pantry closet that had grown unruly during a busy holiday season with lots of entertaining and big meal preparation. It was no longer a walk-in, but a reach-in closet. My frustration spurred me to systemization because I had "organized" the closet many times before, only to see it deteriorate back to chaos. What's needed for this kind of system is a plan and really "thinking through" how a work space or a process is used. Large commercial banks are good examples, as they design the teller and loan officer work areas for maximum efficiency and uniformity. A loan officer should be able to sit at any desk, at any branch, and know exactly where every document is and access it quickly. If you work behind a desk or a workstation, the time invested in creating your own systems will pay-off every day for many years to come.

9. Signs and Labels

The above kind of systemization can't happen without using signs and labels. As you've already read, we have a saying at *Interior Plant Scapes*, (we even have it posted in the pole-barn at the greenhouse) - "Everyone Knows, Where Everything Goes."

If you live alone or run a one-person operation, maybe you don't need signs and labels, but as soon as you introduce person number two, you will. When you use signs and labels in your systems development, if it's two people or two thousand, everyone will know where everything goes. That's another application of organization versus systemization – without signs and labels, your masterfully organized space "goes away" because no one knows what your intention was and "no one knows, where anything goes." Don't blame your staff for a messy work area or for not following the procedure, if you haven't invested in this essential rule.

> *"Everyone Knows, Where Everything Goes."*

Lastly on signs and labels, if you really want your system to stick, invest the extra time and expense to get professionally made ones. Through the years we've used both hand-made and professional – the professional signs and labels get a higher degree of respect and compliance; people take them more seriously. They look great too!

10. Back to Basics

Legend has it that the late great football coach of the Green Bay Packers, Vince Lombardi, would begin every new season of training by saying, "Gentlemen, this is a football." After that introduction, what followed was a back to the basics lesson on "blocking and tackling." These were not raw recruits Lombardi was talking to, but seasoned professionals, many of whom had won championships. Lombardi's career win/loss record is proof enough of the wisdom and necessity of back to the basics training – and systems! If your team doesn't know how to do blocking and tackling, then in reality you can't win football games.

Back to the basics systems development is akin to assuming nothing about the training process and the vision you have for your business operations and customer experience.

Just because it's obvious to you how a thing should be done, do not assume it is obvious to your staff.

If you've been doing your trade or profession for a decade or more, you intuitively and instinctively make hundreds of seemingly small decisions every week. What's second nature to you, aka *unconscious competent* - you're doing it right and don't even know it, is not to some of your staff, maybe not even the veterans. Many of the people on your staff right now are *unconscious incompetent* – not only do they fail to know how to do some key systems, they don't even realize they don't know. It gets worse...*you* don't know what they don't know! You don't know because you've become so familiar with the work, you just assume some of the basics and never thought to include them in the training manual.

For a painful, yet instructive lesson in back to the basics, do a ride along with one of your staff and watch them go about their day. If you have office staff, stand nearby with a document in your hand and pretend to read, or have a fake phone call with your cell phone to your ear and just listen and observe.

It may be painful, but you'll learn what needs to be systemized.

11. Innovate and Improve

If you missed it before, let me just say it once more: "don't just systemize – innovate." Some people believe that the systems development process is solely creating training and procedural manuals. For some businesses that's a huge and monumental step, but if you stop there you're leaving all the opportunity out of the equation. Yes, you want manuals with all your standard operating procedures (SOP's) but even better, you want to transform your business and your service to do it better, and differentiate it from any other option available on earth. The only way to make that kind of alteration is to continually innovate and improve – and then innovate and improve some more. That's how great companies are made and sustained.

You're not looking for the "homerun – outa-the-park," type of innovation, those seldom happen. You want the continuous discipline to create incremental innovations and improvements that over years create impossible to duplicate "process equity."

Process equity is achieved when your business systems and procedures are so valuable that they become an asset. That's right, your systems, be it order fulfillment or sales and marketing systems, become an asset to your business in the same way your building and your equipment is an asset – only more so. More so because process equity is intellectual property and can't be lost in a hurricane or an economic decline. Lastly, in case you missed it earlier, let me share my all-time favorite Drucker quote again, which has been proven time and again in my own life and business experience:

"Because of the nature of business, it has just two functions, and only two. Marketing and innovation. Marketing and innovation make money. Everything else is a cost."

- Peter Drucker

Bonus Rule and Reminder: *"Work On It While You're Working In It."*

With a thankful acknowledgement to Michael Gerber, I share this last rule and guideline for creating and innovating your systems. The most often asked question Gerber would say he had to field was, "how do I find the time to do all this systems creation work?" It is indeed a stretch for most small business people to think of adding another thing to their overly crowded business and life schedule. In addition, at the beginning of the systems creation process it's hard to see any light at the end of the tunnel of chaos you're drowning in. The reward is there, my friend, and the answer is to learn how to "work on your business, *while* you're working in your business doing it."

If you're still a "technician" in any part of your business, be it sales or bookkeeping or order fulfillment, there are ample chances to innovate and improve what you're doing while you're doing it – that's working *On* it while working *In* it.

Most smart phones have both audio notes and voice to text dictation, so take your pick and dictate the step-by-step systems of everything you do, while you're doing it. If you're not the one doing it, follow around one of your staff and dictate what they're doing. If what they're doing looks hard, frustrating or inefficient, there's the opportunity for innovation and improvement.

The working *On* it while you're working *In* it rule is not just for the beginning of the systems development process – it's for...ever!

The Japanese word for improvement is *Kaizen*, or also translated, "change for the best." Kaizen has become synonymous with a management philosophy known as "continuous improvement." The innovation and improvement never stops. Therefore, whenever you find yourself in the position of employee, doing the business of the business, have the mind-set of working *On* it while you're working *In* it.

Ask questions of everything and throw out all the assumptions and tired clichés and worn out belief systems. A good reminder is *that old broken-down belief systems usually get in the way of new break-through business systems.*

CHAPTER 11
Making your Systems Stick

The Systems for the Systems

"What you tolerate, you encourage. What you permit, you promote."

- Unknown

Every once in a while, my wife Crystal and I have a conversation about what it would look like to sell our home and live in a condominium. As you can imagine, because of the winter migration of our snowbirds, the condo lifestyle is hugely popular in Southwest Florida. Some of our friends have opted for it as well, but we hear mixed reviews. If you *go condo* there are some wonderful benefits of amenities and maintenance-free living that are appealing. Club rooms, resort style pools, and fitness centers are just a short walk away, but it's the ability to leave all the up-keep to someone else that sells most people on condo living.

There is, however, another element I've discovered that comes with the whole condominium lifestyle – "the condo-commandos." My friend Bill Smith lives in a lavish high-rise condo just minutes from his work and at my urging has told me the good, the bad, and the ugly of living not just with the amenities and services – but with the people and the rules. The commandos are the people who create a retirement career out of enforcing the rules.

When you sign your mortgage (or lease if you're renting) you're also required to sign a covenant that you've read and agree to the rules and regulations of the condominium. Most condominiums have a management company that has created these rules and standards for life within the community. If you're a free spirit and couldn't imagine someone else dictating your lifestyle, condo life is definitely not for you. Bill told me some of the silly and petty rules he has to abide by. He's allowed to have his own dog, but if his daughter wants to visit and bring her small dog – sorry, no can do.

The flip side of the rules – and this, the point of the story - is that the rules, properly enforced, create an orderly and agreed upon standard within the community. Bill has come to appreciate not just the rules and regulations that govern his condo community, but the property manager who's a stickler for their enforcement, which in turn ensures an efficient and disciplined neighborhood.

What you may not like for your condominium community is exactly what you want for your business. You want a community where the people who work there understand precisely what's expected of them and have agreed to the standards of employment and their position. That sounds simple enough, but if you're a small business leader you know it's not generally the case. Not only do people not know what their job description is (because it's not written down anywhere), they've never really been trained to the standards. The real rub is when staff members know and have been trained, yet simply choose to "do it my way."

When I talk to other small business people about systems, many will say, "Oh, I've tried that and it doesn't work." What they mean is that they couldn't get their people to agree to and abide by the terms of the community (conditions of employment). It is a sad, sad story to see a small business person invest hours (most likely, years) creating systems and procedures for their business only to be deluded by thinking that once done their staff will just automatically abide by them.

There's a lot that could be said about the question, "How do you get your people to want what you want and follow the systems you've created?" The two ideas I want to share will not be exhaustive on this subject, but they've created a new business paradigm that has transformed the way I think about our systems and our people. You see, I was one of those deluded guys who couldn't connect the dots between the systems I created and their full implementation until I understood, first, *what you tolerate, you encourage* – and second, the *deception of the gradual.*

What you tolerate, you encourage...

Recently, I read a story about a teacher complaining to her principal that she didn't like teaching one of her classes because a few students always talked during the class. What the wise principal told her not only changed the way she taught, she said, *"It changed my life."* When the principal told her, "What you tolerate, you encourage," it was like a lightning bolt of truth and she realized she was partly to blame for the students' disruptive behavior. This teacher realized she was responsible for the behavior in her classroom

> ...*what you permit, you promote*

and actually promoting it – by permitting it. These two companion truths – *what you tolerate, you encourage* and *what you permit you promote* – have wide reaching applications for our business and our lives.

When we choose to ignore sloppy work, non-compliance, and laziness we are actually encouraging it. Your staff need to know you are serious about your business and the work it performs to serve others. But not serious as a mean-spirited ogre – serious as in we are professionals who have a commitment to excellence in ourselves and our work.

Here is the great news about the systems development process you're committing to: the very act of designing and creating systems for every detail of your operation is the premier testimony of being serious about your business. By investing the time to create the systems, you're modeling a lifestyle of excellence – in turn, when you tolerate your business being run "any ole way," you're encouraging your staff to think and act the same way.

Strategic Training Objectives Checklist

Now take this truth full circle and connect it to your systems development work – specifically to your Strategic Training Objectives (STO's). We have a training document for STO's for each position that requires the new hire to initialize beside each objective their full understanding and willingness to comply.

It reads like this:

> By initialing, I agree that I understand this aspect of the training for my position as "Plant Care Gardener." I will, to the best of my ability, follow the standards and procedures

as they are outlined in this training manual.

This is a lot like the covenant someone must sign when they move into a condominium community. They are agreeing to comply with the rules and standards as outlined in the document they're signing.

One of the most frustrating things to hear from an employee is, "I didn't know we did it that way." Sometimes it's legit because you the owner or manager didn't take the time to train to the standards, however, many times the comment is a ruse to cover for laziness or incompetence. The beauty of the Strategic Training Objectives Checklist is the written proof that, yes, you did know that's the way we do things and you agreed. The purpose of the checklist is not to have evidence so that you get to wave it in a staff person's face when they screw up – no, it's a document that communicates the seriousness of the work you do and gains agreement at the beginning of the relationship.

Not too long ago, I had one of our delivery and installation guys tell me how much he loved the new system of stabilizing our corn plants (that's a common name for a Draceana that's top-heavy and prone to lean if not properly staked). He learned of the technique in passing from another staff member. His enthusiasm was commendable, but I was far from excited by his comment because the "new system" should have been part of his first week's training and here he was six months in and just now learning it. Obviously he missed that part of the training and his supervisor missed his initials. Unless you commit to the system of a Training Objectives Checklist you have no way to make your systems stick because they're difficult to enforce.

The Strategic Training Objectives Checklist is just one more tool to assure that the systems you've invested in designing are actually "known and understood" by everyone. The checklist adds another layer of "seriousness" to your training and day to day operations. Here are some other ideas as related to The Strategic Training Objectives Checklist:

1. The STO Checklist includes all of the tasks, knowledge, and skills that make up the systems for a particular job position.

2. The STO Checklist becomes a step-by-step training agenda for a new hire.

3. The STO Checklist is a communication tool and safeguard to assure that all of the information about a job position has been transferred from Trainer to Trainee.

4. The STO Checklist includes a space for the Trainer and Trainee to each initial and date that the information has been shared and understood.

5. The STO Checklist is an accountability tool to hold everyone in the company to the standards we have all agreed upon.

6. The STO Checklist is micro-managing the customer experience – so that the vision of the business owner is becoming reality – every time.

7. The STO Checklist is making the systems The Bossy Nag, not another person.

The Deception of the Gradual

When we put a gorgeous new foliage plant into an executive's office not only do we assure them we'll be there to care for all its needs, we also guarantee that if it dies we'll replace it. Actually, it's not "if" – it's "when" it dies, because most of our accounts don't have the ideal conditions for long-term plant growth. The tough part in our plant care system is identifying the when. You see, we never really say the word "die" when referring to a plant – we use a gentler term like decline, because no one wants a dead plant in their office, not even for a day. The trick then is to train the Gardeners when the plant has "declined" to the point that they should submit a work order for its replacement – it's a trick because of The Deception of the Gradual.

The Deception of the Gradual tricks our Gardeners into believing that an ugly plant really isn't ugly because the decline from gorgeous to not-so-much, happened so gradually they were deceived. My working definition for The Deception of the Gradual is: small imperceptible changes occurring over a long period of time that go unnoticed.

It's easy to see the effects of The Deception of the Gradual when you're talking about foliage plants, but perhaps not as easy to see in your business systems. The reality, of course, is that everything in our world, in our lives, and in our business, moves from order to disorder. Without sounding too philosophical, everything and everyone is deteriorating and in the process of decay. Wouldn't it be cool if you messed up your garage and then slowly watched it regain a state of cleanliness and order?

Of course, the exact opposite is true. The Deception of the Gradual explains how we gain an extra 10 or 20 pounds and never really notice, or how once gorgeous homes fall into disrepair and are almost beyond hope. It's also responsible for a loving relationship between a husband and wife, who were soul mates, imperceptibly becoming mere roommates sharing the same home. Unless you're keenly aware of the insidious Deception of the Gradual, what you once prized and worked hard to build will wither into mediocrity or much worse.

How to Combat The Deception of the Gradual

The title of this chapter was The Systems for the System – so here are my best ideas for the tidal wave of forces coming against you and your quest for order. This is how you make your systems stick:

1. Plan with The Deception of the Gradual in Mind

Now that you're aware of this beast that will silently and slowly eat away at your best efforts, plan for it and prepare for it. Yes, optimism and a positive attitude about the future is essential for success, but add to your optimistic plans the systems for keeping the systems intact.

2. Create Margin Days to Reboot the system

In your planning for Tasks, Target Times, and Frequency of Tasks, don't schedule every minute of the week or month. One of the Tasks should be a day to reboot the system. For the *Interior Plant Scapes* greenhouse that means that once a month there is an assigned task (with a system and checklist) for organizing the Pole Barn. As I mentioned earlier, there's a ton of activity in this area for delivery and installations – even with the best systems, the order gradually "goes away." If we didn't create the Margin Day system to regain the order, we lose the efficiency of the space. The reboot day (or half day or whatever the target time is) creates a pause in the normal order fulfillment activity to regain the order and review the systems. For this to work you must schedule it as an appointment, keep the appointment, and follow through on your good intentions

3. Use Meetings as a System Reboot Opportunity

Yes, meetings! Meetings can be a huge time waster, but don't swing the pendulum too far in the opposite direction and throw them out completely. Regular meetings are like personal hygiene for the deception of the gradual. Read a good book on meetings or learn how to make yours productive, effective - and fun. Do not, I repeat, do not use your meeting time as a pity-party to gripe and complain that no one is following your systems. Share the vision of the company (again and again) and the vision of each department and find creative ways to link the systems with their fulfillment.

4. One-On-One Meetings

If one person on your staff is going astray and shows an inability to embrace some aspect of their work, DO NOT make it a topic for the all staff meeting. Sit down with "that" employee and talk about what's going on. One-on-one meetings should be regularly scheduled as an opportunity to have face time with the boss or a supervisor. Ask good questions and you'll get good feedback about their work – and their lives. This is hard to make happen as part of a busy company, but it's an investment in your people that you'll come to appreciate.

5. On-Going Training

Another topic for meetings is training. When your people are engaged in their work, they'll naturally want to learn more to be better at their jobs. This is another way to demonstrate that you're serious about your systems – and if you're serious, your people will be too. Training does not have to always be about new information. Repetition is an aid to learning and some of the core ideas of your business must be repeated – repeated more than you would ever think.

6. Quality Assurance Department

Quality is something that every business talks about but very few have a department to *assure* that it happens! Yes the whole systems development process in which you've engaged is about creating quality, but this chapter is the reality-check to ensure your systems stick. Maybe you've heard that "Quality is not a department," but I disagree. Yes, the commitment to quality must be the DNA of every department and staff member, but someone's job description must include quality assurance inspections. Because people are people, they will do what's *expected* when they know it will be *inspected*. The quality assurance department should make liberal use of checklists and follow up.

7. A Fresh Set of Eyes

The quality assurance must be performed by someone other than the person doing the work. Because of The Deception of the Gradual, you need a fresh set of eyes! A fresh set of eyes is someone who's not under the spell of the deception – the deception that the work I'm doing is perfectly acceptable, when in fact it went off the rails miles back. If you go back to my first example, our Gardeners prune and trim dead and dying leaves as part of the regular plant care. If you prune just one or two leaves each week you may not see the gradual decline. A quality assurance person, with a fresh set of eyes, will see plainly what has become almost invisible.

The Double-Whammy that Kills Your Systems

Up until this time, maybe you thought it's OK to let a lot of the small things slide. When you combine these two concepts you can quickly surmise how your best efforts to make changes in your business failed. Teach your people how The Deception of the Gradual can trip them in their work and their life. It's not the huge egregious errors in judgment you need to fear, but the small and almost imperceptible slip-ups and omissions over time. Because the slip-ups are ignored and tolerated, the behavior is encouraged.

With that in mind, let me lead into the last chapter by asking, "Are you really serious about your systems?" and, "Are you serious enough to take the narrow path that will get you to a business that works?"

CHAPTER 12

The Narrow Road to a Business that Works

Entering the funnel backwards

"Entrepreneurship is living a few years of your life like most people won't, so that you can spend the rest of your life like most people can't"

- **Anonymous**

"Small is the gate and narrow the road that leads to life and only a few find it."

- **Jesus of Nazareth**

This had to be the all-time best sermon illustration I had ever seen. My pastor was holding a very large funnel – the kind used for adding transmission fluid to an engine. This funnel was extra-large on top and then narrowed to a small hole on the bottom to fit into tight openings. He said, as he held the funnel high for all to see, "The most successful lives are lived by entering the funnel backwards!" It was a great picture of doing the contrary thing and choosing the road less traveled – the narrow road.

Most people (business people included) choose what seems to be the easier road because it's wide and that's where everyone is going, so it must be right. The big idea my pastor was introducing is that our choices early on in life have far reaching implications for success or failure. The analogy of the funnel has great applications both for our personal development and for building a systems driven business.

Entering the funnel backwards

If you want to build an amazing life for the long term, the choices at the beginning are limited and may seem hard, restrictive, and uncomfortable – like entering a funnel backwards. For example, to get an education (not just a grade) you have to skip a lot of the parties, video gaming, and TV shows everyone else is choosing, so that you can study. This cramps your style and the choices really limit your freedom and your fun. Entering the funnel backwards is restrictive and hard – at first! Let me say that last part again, "at first!" As you progress through the funnel it starts to open up and become easier – there is more room and freedom...more success! Listen friend, building a systems driven business requires the same kind of discipline.

Choosing the narrow path to a systems driven business

At the beginning of your business development journey you're going to have to work hard and make tough choices that limit your options in the way you do business. If you enter your business journey on the broad road and do business any-ole-way it may indeed seem easier, but believe me when I say it is only easier at first. That broad road leads to a business that consumes your life. That journey leads to a business that is more like a job and actually worse than a job because, to roughly paraphrase the Eagles, "you can't clock out anytime you like – and you can't ever leave." You cannot do business this way and yet expect meaningful success. One dimensional success is no success at all.

If you've read this far, it's obvious you're ready to be one of the few that choose the narrow road. The narrow road that feels uncomfortable and restrictive "at first," will reward you later with a business and a life that many dream of, but only a few achieve. If the narrow road to a business that works is about making choices, what exactly are the choices you must make? These are the questions I wish someone would have asked me 30 years ago when I was beginning my business journey.

Will you choose to think differently about your business?

Think about your business *apart from you and not a part of you!* You'll never achieve the beautiful benefits of a systems driven business if you believe the whole thing has to depend on you to make it happen. Think about your business – visualize your business operating in the hands of others who have been equipped with your systems strategy. The reason many business people say they hate employees or pretend to only want a small business is because they have not learned how to create systems. They have tried to delegate the work of their business and it went horribly wrong – they were burned and embarrassed.

The transformation begins when you change the way you think about your business. Read that again about seven more times or until you really get it inside you in a deep and personal way. If you're choosing the narrow path, visualize your business in the capable hands of your staff. These people are capable because you've **equipped them** with the tools to get amazing results.

Will you choose to equip your people and not just encourage them?

One of the most over-used words today in our *coaching* obsessed business world is "encourage." If you were going on a very long journey, would you rather be encouraged or equipped? You can choose the "attaboys" and the "you-can-do-it" encouragement, or the tools and equipment, the maps and skills, and the systems that give you the confidence to succeed. Encouragement has its place, but only after someone has been completely and thoroughly equipped!

Your narrow path to business success includes the hard and intentional work of not just delegating a task, but of creating the system and training (and training some more) so that your entire team is equipped for every task in the business. If your business coach thinks all you need is more encouragement, find a coach that'll give you the tools to innovate, invent, and create a turn-key business revolution.

Will you choose to create a Vision for your life – then for your business?

The narrow road journey will require a vision big enough and powerful enough to keep you going when you're weary or tempted to give up. I was sitting by a guy named John on a plane and he asked what I was writing (I was writing this chapter). We struck up a conversation about business and he told me his goal for his business was to save enough money so his wife and kids could enjoy great vacations. John told me the story of a busy CPA firm that wanted his computer-tech services. The caveat with this potential client was they wanted 24/7 access to him from January to May, and 30 minute-or-less on-site service calls if the problem couldn't be solved remotely. To his credit, he said no. He had decided upon the life he wanted for himself (and his family) and was now aligning his business to create that life. Perhaps, the next step for John is a vision of his business that doesn't include him as a computer tech and then he can take vacations whenever he wants. If he does choose this, it's a different path. The narrow path to a business that works without the owner requires a big vision and a lot of emotional reasons why. Your vision must include your reasons why.

Will you choose to fall in love with systems?

Don't just fall in love with systems - become a systems junkie. Read and learn about systems, innovation, reengineering, and franchise prototypes operations. Become obsessed with everything you can learn about great companies that have transformed the way we do business in America: McDonald's, Holiday Inn, Fed-Ex, Starbucks – companies that have created a predictable customer experience, because they've created predictable systems.

Reread Chapter 2 – Systems Create Order from Chaos, and go looking for order. Whenever you see order in a business – (generally in the form of an amazing customer experience), go into research-mode and uncover the systems behind the order. Then see if there's an application for you to use the system in your business. When I took my car in for service at a major dealership, they used a 21-point checklist form – for each of the items there was a green box, a yellow box, or a red box. A checkmark in the green box meant that item was OK, yellow meant, "Caution, will need service soon," and red indicated, "Service needed now." Well, as you can guess, that form was adapted for *Interior Plant Scapes* and our quality assurance system uses a very similar checklist – except we evaluate plants instead of cars. Be a student of systems. Systems are beautiful things and properly used will create amazing results.

Will you choose to become the intelligent designer of your business?

Remember that systems are the sign of intelligent design. You can create a memorable, predictable, and profitable customer experience by choosing to be the intelligent designer of your business. You can create order and you can duplicate the success by replicating the process. If you will choose to be the intelligent designer of your business you will "think-through" the entire customer experience. The intelligent designer creates an amazing customer experience and micro-manages every detail of it, so that nothing is left to chance. Don't settle for the broad road of mediocrity for your business. Don't do business just like everyone else. Choose to create a business that serves people in a special and elegant way, no matter what it is you do. This will require some hard work on your part. You won't stumble upon the amazing innovations and systems that create your stellar business by accident. They will come as you experiment and start trying new things. It always amazes me how we can continue to improve small processes, year after year, as we try new things and challenge the status quo.

Unlocking the Secrets of Your Business

Pay close attention to what I'm about to share with you. I would like to conclude with a personal story and one of the most profound lessons I have ever learned. The lesson first, then the story. *Your business has untapped potential in it that's just waiting to be discovered and invented – ideas and innovations not yet revealed that could transform your entire business and perhaps your entire industry.* This is very personal for me because I learned this at a time when I was very close to giving up on my business and just selling it and getting out. One Sunday morning I was journaling about different options of things I could do if I sold my business and pursued something else. In a flash of insight, I was reminded of a story I'd read in the biography of George Washington Carver. The book was in my personal library so I got up and read it again.

Carver who was born a slave in the late 1800s. Carver had the unique opportunity to get an education (which he credits as Divine providence) and combined his natural love and affinity for plants with a degree in botany. He was not only a scholar, but a scientist who experimented with plants and soil. Carver was one of the first to understand the benefits of crop rotation.

Through his extensive research, he discovered that crop after crop of cotton was depleting the soil of essential nutrients. Many farmers took his advice and planted crops of peanuts which replenished the soil. The result was bumper crops of peanuts, but no market to sell them. Carver felt the tension and ridicule of many people suffering under the weight of his advice. The following is a personal account from his autobiography:

I retreated into my lab. Only there could I avoid the faces of my students and friends. Only there could I be alone.

> *"Dear Mr. Creator, why did you make the peanut?"*

But somehow I was not alone. Even in the silence and stillness, I felt another presence. Falling to my knees, I begged understanding from my Savior and Creator.

And as I prayed, I was drawn to my feet. Out of the lab I went, into the nearby woodlands and fields. "Oh Mr. Creator," I asked, "Why did you make this Universe?"

"Your little mind asks too much," came the answer, "Ask something more your size."

Then, "What was man made for?" I asked.

"You are still asking too much, little man. Try once more." I fell to my knees.

"Dear Mr. Creator, why did you make the peanut?"

"Now you are asking questions your own size. Together we will find the answers."

Carver cried out for the secrets to the peanut. Who would have thought there was untapped potential in the humble little peanut? Through experimentation and hard work, Carver discovered over 250 uses for the peanut: cosmetics, pesticides, rubber, plastics, axle grease...and of course most importantly, peanut butter.

On that Sunday morning, when I was ready to give my business up, I was reminded of this story and started asking The Creator for the secrets to the Interiorscape business I was in. "Show me the secrets to this business and this industry," I asked, "and help me to create the systems and innovations for amazing breakthroughs."

That day was a turning point for me, as I began to understand that the opportunities for innovations, inventions, and re-inventions were endless.

I was renewed and reenergized to go to work "on" my business to create something unique – to become the intelligent designer of the systems that would serve our customers in an amazing way. And by serving our customers this way, serve my life and my vision.

> **Ask the Creator for the break-through systems and innovations for your business.**

Listen carefully, in the same way there is untapped potential in your business just waiting to be discovered. No matter how "ordinary" you believe your business to be, chances are there are industry changing opportunities latent within it. *You* can cry out in the same way Carver did and ask the Creator for the secrets of your business and industry, you can ask for the break-through ideas and innovations that will revolutionize your company. Now you can take those ideas and create a systems strategy so that you can implement them into your business and customer experience. An idea or innovation that, not implemented is worthless.

Yes, that Sunday morning was big for me, because I saw the opportunity to transform my business and my life – not just with new ideas and innovations but with the ability to harness the power of systems to implement them. It was another confirmation that I could have victory over my business. You too can experience and enjoy the same kind of victory over your business – you too can transform your business and your life. You can enjoy the victory that goes to the business with superior systems.

Acknowledgments

In this, my first book, I share a lot about the path out of the chaos and mess of my business start-up, and for that journey there are many to whom I'm deeply indebted.

On the business side, I'd like to thank Michael Gerber for his book, The E-Myth - it was the break-through that gave me a new belief-system about my business.

He's helped thousands of small business men and women have - "not just a business, but a life."

Dan Kennedy, Rich Harshaw and Jay Abraham are probably the smartest marketing guys on the planet - I've read and listened to them for years. Interior Plant Scapes has been my laboratory for testing and implementing their marketing advice for which I am forever grateful! Once the systems were in place, their training in marketing gave me confidence to go to the next level. Marketing is so vital to business success that my next book is titled: *Victory Goes to the Business with Superior "Marketing" Systems.*

Through the years I've been deeply influenced by the great motivational teachers and personal development masters, but two stand out. First, Earl Nightingale and his *Lead the Field* program ingrained in me the importance of attitude and right thinking. I wore out my first copy of Lead the Field on cassettes and then my second copy on CD's. In addition, Earl's "The Strangest Secret" audio recording is the perennial classic.

Second is Zig Ziglar, who taught not just motivational truths, but solid sales training. He was the first businessman I met who beautifully articulated and integrated his Christian faith with his business principles and goals: "if you believe your business (product/service) is the best, you have a moral obligation to sell it well."

Also on the business side I'd like to thank Christian Burch and Tim Jacobs, my editors, for their enthusiastic spirit for this project, and Lynn Schneider who improves everything she touches – can't wait to see what you "touch" next!

On the personal side, the man who invested not only in my business life, but also in my spiritual life is Dave Moreland. When I asked him, "How is it possible to have a passion for Christ **and** for my business'" there was not a better question I could have asked in all the world – or a more perfect person to answer it. His answers came during a three year mentoring relationship with one-on-one weekly breakfast meetings. The training and friendship continued in the mountains of North Carolina. He and his wife Shirley are responsible for giving us 'the North Carolina bug" by hosting us in their mountain home.

The only man who impacted me more – up close and personal – was my Dad. He not only gave me my *entrepreneurial assumption* ("of course I'm going to have my own business"), he generously allowed me to start my business in the front office of his printing company. Because my desk was in earshot of his, I learned superior telephone skills by listening to him talk with prospects and customers. Thank You Dad for your love and support all these years – I love you!

The *woman* who deserves the most acknowledgment for "our" journey is of course my wife, Crystal. Her faith, love and belief in me is as oxygen. Her support begins even before the *Interior Plant Scapes* start-up, as I told her my idea for a plant business while we were in Orlando for a chef's convention – getting vendor ideas for my catering business. She married me regardless of my flakiness. Her joy when I told her about getting every new account made me work that much harder – and her love when I was discouraged made the next day possible.

Lastly, on the spiritual side, I must acknowledge God and my faith in Jesus Christ. Redemption through faith in Christ is a real thing – it's the only explanation for the life-changing experience I had at 22 years old. God "turned all my lights on" after I made a decision for Him one day in church – the desire to learn, read and study was instant and transformed my life. Growing a small business is the ultimate tool in the hands of God to build character and dependence on Him.

CPSIA information can be obtained at www.ICGtesting.com
Printed in the USA
LVOW01s1335120215

426749LV00003B/2/P